A CREATIVE STEP-BY-STEP GUIDE TO

PATIO
GARDENING

A CREATIVE STEP-BY-STEP GUIDE TO

PATIO
GARDENING

Author
Sue Phillips

Photographer
Neil Sutherland

▲ AURA BOOKS

CLB 3313
This edition published in 1997 by Aura Books
© 1994 CLB International, Godalming, Surrey
Printed and bound in Singapore
All rights reserved
ISBN 1-85833-164-1

Credits
Edited and designed: Ideas into Print
Photographs: Neil Sutherland
Photographic location: Russell's Garden Center, Sussex
Typesetting: Ideas into Print and Ash Setting and Printing
Production Director: Gerald Hughes
Production: Ruth Arthur, Sally Connolly, Neil Randles

THE AUTHOR

Sue Phillips began gardening at the age of four, encouraged
by her grandfather, and had her first greenhouse at eleven,
where she grew a collection of cacti and propagated all
sorts of plants. After leaving school, she worked for a year
on a general nursery before studying horticulture at
Hadlow College of Agriculture & Horticulture, Kent for
three years. For the next five years, she was co-owner and
manager of a nursery in Cambridgeshire, before joining a
leading garden products company as Gardens Adviser.
This involved answering gardening queries, handling
complaints, writing articles and press releases, speaking at
gardening events and broadcasting for local radio. In 1984,
she turned freelance and since then she has contributed
regularly to various gardening and general interest
magazines and has appeared often on radio and TV
programs. She is the author of seven published books. She
lives in a very windy village on the south coast of England
near Chichester and has a very intensively cultivated
quarter-acre cottage garden on solid clay, plus a vegetable
garden next door, which she looks after with help from her
husband and hindrance from a Persian cat.

THE PHOTOGRAPHER

Neil Sutherland has more than 25 years experience in a
wide range of photographic fields, including still-life,
portraiture, reportage, natural history, cookery, landscape
and travel. His work has been published in countless books
and magazines throughout the world.

Half-title page: Conifers and hostas in a sheltered corner.
Title page: Laying the foundations for a successful patio.
Copyright page: A summer display reflected on the patio.

CONTENTS

Introduction	10-11	Heathers and conifers	62-63
What makes a patio?	12-13	The patio in spring	64-65
Laying slabs on sand with mortar	14-15	The patio in summer	66-67
Slabs on sand with dry mortar	16-17	Herbaceous patio plants	68-69
Laying bricks on sand	18-19	A cottage garden feature	70-71
Laying bricks on mortar	20-21	A Mediterranean display	72-73
Laying cobbles in mortar	22-23	A scented pot for the patio	74-75
An ornamental feature in a gravel area	24-25	Planting up a patio rose	76-77
Using stones and gravel as a decorative feature	26-27	A selection of patio roses	78-79
		A potted rock garden	80-81
Planting in the cracks between slabs	28-29	Rock plants on the patio	82-83
Planting up beds in paving	30-31	Herbs for the patio	84-85
Ideas for plants and paving	32-33	Planting a cherry tree in a patio container	86-87
Wooden decking	34-35		
A water feature in a tub	36-37	Fruit and vegetables on the patio	88-89
Small water features	38-39	Hydrangeas - ideal for a shady patio	90-91
Larger water features	40-41	Flowering shrubs for the patio	92-93
Walls and raised beds	42-43	An evergreen shrub in an oak barrel	94-95
Creating a small hanging basket	44-45	Exotic plants in a wicker basket	96-97
A mixed hanging basket	46-47	Grasses in terracotta	98-99
A classic hanging basket	48-49	An oriental-style display	100-101
Hanging baskets for a patio display	50-51	Bonsai on the patio	102-103
A vivid wall basket to take the eye	52-53	Patio furniture	104-105
Planting a clematis in a patio container	54-55		
Trellis on the patio	56-57		
Climbers for the patio	58-59		
Containers on patios	60-61	Index and credits	106-108

A PATIO - THE OUTDOOR ROOM

A patio is often described as an outdoor room, but it is actually halfway between the house and the garden, containing elements of both. From indoors, there are the furniture, floor coverings and potted plants; while from outdoors there is the weather, which means that you need to use plants, surfacing and 'hardware' durable enough to withstand the climate.

This book focuses on patio gardening, with advice on which plants to use, how to plant and care for them, and how to team them together - both with each other and with 'hard' patio fittings, such as paving, walls and containers - to create interesting planting schemes.

Patios need not always be the contemporary style suntraps we have come to expect. The basic idea can be adapted to suit houses and gardens of very different styles, simply by using appropriate combinations of paving, screening, furniture and plants. The patio does not even have to be next to the house; if the only place that gets the sun in the evening is down the garden, there is no reason why you should not have your patio there. Conversely, if you prefer to keep out of the sun, you could create a cool shady patio - perhaps using a Mediterranean-style roof of vines.

A patio provides a unique gardening environment that makes it possible to grow many kinds of slightly tender or delicate plants, usually sunlovers, that may prove difficult or unsatisfactory when grown in the open garden. There is also the opportunity to make full use of plants in containers and beds or on walls to soften the hard lines of a patio. So, whether you use plants to decorate the patio, or the patio to house your favorite plants, you will be spoilt for choice!

Left: A relaxing place to sit and enjoy the view.   *Right: An arum lily crowns a terracotta patio container.*

What makes a patio?

Patios can be made in all sorts of styles to suit their locations, but whichever you choose, the design should be inviting, easy to use and maintain, and suitable for the people who will use it. Plants on a family patio are generally easiest to manage if they are grouped together, rather than randomly dotted about, and this is also the way to make a good display from only a few plants. Most commonly, people only think of growing plants in containers or hanging baskets, but decorative though they are, there are many other options, including beds let into the paving, or made where single paving slabs have been removed. You can even grow plants in the cracks between paving slabs. Many possibilities are explored on the following pages.

In addition to providing shelter, brickwork 'stores' heat from the sun and helps keep the patio warm in the evening. It also makes a good neutral background for colorful plants in containers.

Ivy is self-clinging, but will not damage a well-built wall; being evergreen, the effect remains all year - variegated kinds are colorful.

Above: *Pots, wall planters, climbers and a patio pond with a fountain and marginal plants all add interest to a sheltered, sunny seating area that looks good, yet is quick and easy to maintain in good condition.*

Drought-tolerant alpines look good surrounded by pebbles, which act as a mulch that suppresses weeds and slows water evaporation from the soil.

Light-colored paving reflects heat and light, helping to create the 'suntrap' effect of a patio. Textured surfaces are safest in wet conditions.

Grow colorful annuals in tubs, hanging baskets and beds. When summer is over, replace them with hardy, spring-flowering plants.

Below: *A patio designed for luxurious leisure time. A parasol over a table cuts down the glare if you are eating outdoors. Leave enough space around patio furniture and items such as a barbecue so that people can move around them easily and in safety.*

Trellis is a useful way of enclosing a patio, providing light shade, shelter or privacy. Use it to grow climbers or hang wall planters.

Furniture is as much part of the landscape of the patio as the plants are, so choose a style that reflects that of the house and garden.

For a coordinated look keep to one style of containers and, if possible, match them to the furniture, paving or walls surrounding the patio.

Water features on or next to a patio are very relaxing. There is always something to watch - dragonflies, fish, or perhaps a fountain. The shallow edges attract birds to drink.

Conifers and variegated evergreens planted on or near the patio provide easy-care interest throughout the year

Above: *Shelter and privacy are essential for a good patio. A small area enclosed by trellis and climbers with a pergola and hanging baskets makes a cosy place to sit out.*

Gravel is a good alternative to hard paving, but can be a nuisance if used close to the house, as it gets trodden indoors.

Laying slabs on sand with mortar

Preparation is the secret of sound paving - expect it to take at least as long as actually laying the slabs. Do not lay paving slabs straight onto the soil, because rain water will get under them, making the soil soft and muddy. The slabs will then sink in, wearing depressions in the soil and causing the slabs to rock. The paving soon becomes uneven and can be dangerous if the slabs tip up. To prevent this happening, prepare a proper 'base' before you lay any slabs. It need not be very deep, as a patio or path will not have to carry much weight. Start by leveling and consolidating the ground. You may need to excavate a few inches of soil for the base, leaving only the paving visible above ground. Alongside a house wall, leave a gap of 6in(15cm) between the surface of the finished paving and the dampproof course in the wall. If laying a patio, whether it be adjacent to the house or free-standing, leave the ground sloping very slightly so the water runs off it. A slope of 1in(2.5cm) in 4ft(1.2m) is all that is needed.

1 *After raking the sand roughly level, smooth the surface by drawing a length of wood over it. This leaves it evenly firmed down without consolidating it too much.*

A 2in(5cm) layer of rubble with 1-2in(2.5-5cm) of building sand on top makes an adequate base for a patio.

2 *Suitable mortar for laying bricks is available ready-mixed in bags. Make up a small quantity of mortar with water as directed and place five small blobs onto the sand base before laying each slab on top. Each blob should be about the size of a large tablespoonful.*

A wooden framework holds everything together until it sets.

3 *Position each slab carefully before putting it down so that you lay it accurately, without disturbing the sand or mortar underneath. Tap wooden pegs about 0.4in(1cm) thick between the slabs as spacers.*

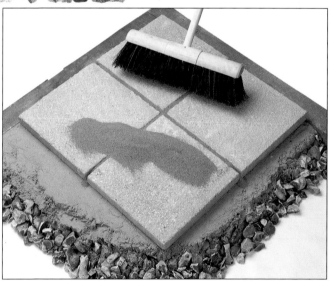

4 *Lightly tap down the slab with the handle of a club hammer to bed it in. Lay the wood across to check that it lies flush with adjacent slabs and use a spirit level to check that it is level.*

5 *Work methodically, regularly checking levels as you progress. When all the slabs are laid, remove the spacer pegs and brush dried sand into the gaps between the slabs.*

15

Slabs on sand with dry mortar

There are some situations where fixed paving slabs are neither necessary nor desirable. If you think you may want to alter the patio layout later, perhaps taking up some slabs to make a sunken bed or pond, then it will be easier if you only have to lift the slabs. Slabs in such an area can simply rest in place while those around them are mortared down permanently. If you use very large heavy slabs, cement may not be necessary at all, especially if the patio surface will not take much weight. Even if they are not cemented down, you can still fill the cracks between the slabs with mortar to stop weeds growing. Later on you can remove the slabs with a crowbar after chipping the mortar loose; clean up the edges before reusing the slabs. Alternatively, leave the cracks between slabs open, perhaps filled with gravel, and sow rock plants between them. To prepare the site for laying slabs, proceed as described for laying paving slabs on page 14-15, using crushed rubble or ballast covered by building sand, raked firm and leveled. Leave a 6in(15cm) gap between the dampproof course in the house wall and the planned upper surface of the patio, and allow a very slight slope away from the house to deflect water during heavy rain.

1 Lay the slabs a finger's width apart - you can tap in wooden pegs as temporary spacers. Brush dry mortar into the cracks.

Make sure everything is dry at this stage so that the dry mortar runs freely into the cracks.

2 Water briskly with a fine rose. This washes the mortar in, wets it enough so it can set, and cleans the slabs.

3 This method is very easy to do and leaves the slabs clean; the alternative - pushing wet mortar down between the cracks - takes ages and makes a terrible mess.

Below: *The surface of this patio has been kept interesting by varying the pattern of the slabs and letting in the occasional block of bricks or small planting pocket, here featuring lilies and hostas. A wooden deck and steps provide a stylish change of level.*

Right: *Simple paving slabs neatly laid provide an ideal patio surface that sets off plants in beds and containers. Here, the bold, white-edged leaves of Hosta crispula planted in a bed alongside the patio contrast superbly with the warm tones of the slabs.*

Carefully placed containers act as focal points to break up the horizontal symmetry of a patio.

Hostas and other moisture-loving plants have their 'feet' in a damp waterside bed on the other side of the patio.

Laying bricks on sand

Laying bricks involves very much the same technique as used for slabs. Prepare the base of rubble topped with building sand in exactly the same way. The bricks can be secured in place with blobs of mortar, as shown on page 14-15 for paving slabs, except that two blobs of mortar are enough for a brick. However, since bricks are smaller and thicker and less likely to slide about or rock than slabs, they can be laid loose and directly onto the sand. This is a good idea if you think you may want to move them later - perhaps remove some to open up beds or alter the shape of the paved area. It is also rather quicker to make a hard surface in this way than when using mortar, but the result is not quite as durable. Bricks laid straight into sand are most suitable for surfacing a paved area that will not get a lot of heavy traffic over it. Since the bricks are not held in place with mortar, it is also a good idea to check them periodically and re-sit any that seem to have sunk or become uneven. This is most likely to happen in high rainfall areas or where heavy wheelbarrows, etc., are frequently pushed over the area and the weight bears unevenly over the bricks. However, used as intended, it is a perfectly good surface.

Use both hands to lift bricks straight into place. Sit them squarely onto the sand; do not drop one end or it makes a depression that will make the finish uneven.

1 Lay the base layers of 2in(5cm) of rubble and 1-2in(2.5-5cm) of building sand, as shown on pages 14-15. Rake the sand level and firm it down lightly with the back of a rake.

2 Check that the surface is level using a spirit level resting on a flat piece of wood, and smooth the surface over with this so that the sand becomes smooth and consistently firm.

3 Decide on a pattern in which to lay the bricks; these are laid in alternate pairs. Practice laying bricks on a hard surface, away from the prepared base, to gain confidence.

Right: When the brickwork is completed and dry, tip a few buckets of dry sand onto it and smooth it into the cracks with a soft broom. The sand slides into the gaps easily.

The pattern shown here is herringbone, one of the most popular and easy to lay.

4 Tap each brick lightly down at both ends with the handle of a club hammer so that it beds into the sand layer and ends up with the top completely flush with the bricks next to it.

This kiln-dried joint filling sand is very fine, and trickles through the smallest gaps.

5 As you work, check constantly with a spirit level resting on top of a length of wood to make certain that the bricks are completely level. If necessary, add or remove a little sand.

Laying bricks on mortar

A frequently used patio or path needs a hard surface that stays firm in all weathers, is non-slip when frosty or wet and will not sink or tip. It should be strong enough to withstand the weight of a loaded wheelbarrow, patio furniture, etc. - although it will not need the deep foundations required to support the weight of a car. Some of the most popular surfacing for such areas are paving slabs and bricks bedded onto mortar. Bricks create a more interesting texture than many inexpensive types of paving. You can reuse secondhand bricks from old buildings for paths and paved areas, after chipping the old mortar from them, but it is also possible to buy new bricks that resemble old ones. These are useful to create the traditional look of a cottage garden path or paving. Modern bricks are available in a variety of styles and colors to suit other schemes. Bricks can be laid in a wide range of patterns - books and magazines will give you plenty of ideas - but whichever you choose, practice first. With some patterns, even apparently simple ones, it is surprisingly tricky to place adjacent bricks right first time, especially when you are anxious to get them down before the mortar starts to set. For peace of mind, do jobs that involve concreting during spells of mild weather when it is unlikely to rain; extremes of heat or cold will affect concrete. Mortar is available in bags ready to use - just mix it with water. A slightly wet mix is easier to work with and gives you marginally longer to work before it starts to set.

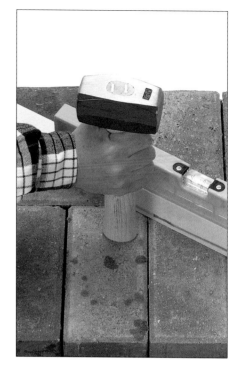

3 Allow a gentle slope (1in/2.5cm in 4ft/1.2m) across the area of bricks, so that rain water runs off. If working next to a wall or the house, make sure the slope takes water away from it.

1 Surround the working area with wooden formwork nailed roughly together. Pour about 1in(2.5cm) of mortar mix over a 2in(5cm) gravel base on flattened and trampled soil.

2 Lay the first row of bricks, firm lightly down and check that the tops are level. Tap down uneven bricks with the handle of a club hammer.

Cleaning the patio

Keep the patio free of dirt and debris to deter weeds and moss colonizing it. They do not just grow in soil between slabs and bricks, but also in organic debris trapped in crevices, even over the top of cement. Clean patios with a stiff brush and warm water with a drop of mild detergent in it, or use a high-pressure hose, taking care not to blow weak mortar out from between the cracks. Do not use bleach, as it can cause discoloration. You can also use persistent path weedkillers on a clean patio in spring to prevent weed growth for the rest of the season.

4 Once all the bricks are in place, brush dry mortar mix into the gaps between the bricks. It is worth filling these hairline cracks to prevent weeds or moss invading the spaces.

5 Use a rose on the spout of a watering can to give the bricks a brief shower. This washes the mortar into the cracks and enables it to set without staining the top of the bricks.

Above: Visually 'break up' a large area of paving by varying the surface pattern, texture or color. Here, a regular pattern of paving slabs has been set amongst bricks to add detail.

Left: You can create all kinds of interesting effects using bricks. Patterns such as these that echo the shape of containers or furniture on the patio can be particularly effective.

Right: Bricks, especially dark red ones, associate particularly well with plants and foliage. Where possible, use them so that plants can spill over and create pleasing contrasts.

21

Laying cobbles in mortar

Cobblestones make a most attractive contrast to areas of flat paving. Use them in place of an occasional slab to add a change of texture. In larger areas, they can add decorative detail or an interesting surface. Because rounded cobblestones are not very comfortable or easy to walk on, they can be used to good effect on a patio to guide people away from overhanging plants or to deter children from getting too close to a barbecue area or pond. Cobbles team specially well with stone seats and ornaments and look superb in an oriental style area. They also make an attractive base on which to stand containers of plants, particularly shrubs - the texture of cobbles associates particularly well with subjects such as Japanese maples and conifers that have feathery foliage. When cobblestones are used as a decorative surfacing amongst plants, it is usual to bed them loosely into the soil; this allows rain water to run through, and also lets you change the design without difficulty. However, if people are to walk on the cobbles, bed them into cement or mortar to hold them firmly in place. Since they can be slippery when wet, it is also a good idea to set cobbles so that about half of each stone is above the level of the cement base, leaving plenty of drainage space for water to run away between the stones. In a large area, lay cobbles on a very slight slope, the same as for paving slabs, so that water does not lie in puddles.

Weeds and moss

Dig out weeds with a narrow-bladed knife or eradicate them using a proprietary path weed-killer. This will kill any plant it touches, so take care to keep it off plants overhanging the paving or deliberately planted in it. Remove large weeds by hand first, as woody top growth persists even after it is dead. Where there is any open soil for plants, weeds can grow, too. Do not use path weedkillers round them as they will kill the plants as well. Weedkillers will not kill moss, nor is it a good idea to use proprietary mosskillers unless they specifically state that they can be used on paving - most do not. Dig out moss with an old knife or trowel instead.

1 Make a boundary of wooden formwork around the working area and nail it together. Pour in about 2in(5cm) of rather wet mortar mix and smooth with a bricklaying trowel.

2 Choose even-sized cobbles, 2-3in (5-7.5cm) in diameter, and press them about halfway down into the mortar. Stagger the rows slightly so that adjacent cobbles fit close together.

3 Work a small area at a time. Continue adding more stones until you have filled the area completely. Try to keep the surface of the cobbles as level as possible as you work.

Left: *A decorative inset made of pebbles within a larger area of paving. Instead of being laid to give the traditional cobbled yard effect, the stones on this patio have been angled to produce a swirling pattern.*

Below: *In this oriental-style area, complete with an appropriate stone lantern, flattish stones have been laid on their sides. This creates a cobbled area that is easier to walk on than one where the stones are set on end.*

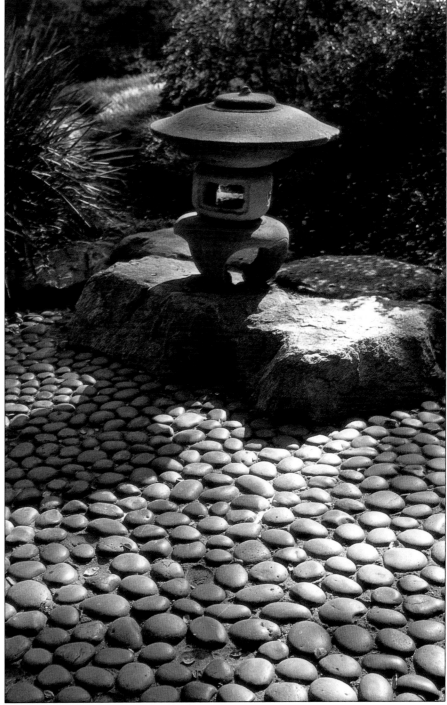

4 *Check the level by laying a piece of wood over the top; gently tap any uneven cobbles into place with a club hammer. Do not tap the cobbles directly; they may split.*

Be sure to check the level and tap down the stones before the mortar starts to set.

An ornamental feature in a gravel area

Gravel is the cheapest, yet one of the most attractive, paths you can have. It is also the quickest and easiest to put down or to take up and move. It is good for home security, as the crunching sound it makes underfoot gives warning of visitors. Gravel is very adaptable and looks 'at home' in a rustic cottage garden or an ultramodern 'designer' patio. But one of its best features is the way plants take to it. Seedlings quickly naturalize themselves or you can deliberately plant into it. The most suitable plants for growing in gravel are naturally drought-resistant alpines, herbs, euphorbias, and small shrubs such as cistus, helianthemum and hebe. Conifers associate marvelously with gravel, but many will go brown around the edges if subjected to drought. Junipers are the most tolerant; choose a compact variety if space is limited. Gravel can also make a stunning feature with a patio. Try leaving out a few paving slabs to create an irregular area of bed and make a planted gravel garden in the space. Team some suitable plants together, and perhaps add an ornament - it looks good, yet is virtually maintenance-free.

Laying gravel on a rubble foundation

Alternatively, gravel can be laid over a base of rubble. If you have some broken bricks or other domestic rubble, you could use this, as long as the pieces are no larger than 2x2in(5x5cm), otherwise they will 'appear' through the gravel. As some of the gravel will sink between the larger pieces of rubble, make sure that the gravel layer is at least 2in(5cm) deep so that it covers the rubble completely.

3 To make a planting hole, sweep aside some gravel and cut a cross in the fabric, about twice the width of the rootball of the plant you are inserting.

Anti-weed mulch material is a flexible plastic fabric, often sold cut to length off a roll in garden centers.

1 After leveling and consolidating the soil, cover it with anti-weed mulch material for a maintenance-free gravel area. Simply unroll the fabric and lay it out over the ground.

2 When the fabric is in place, cover it with gravel to hold it down or pinion it with wire 'hairpins'. Use a rake to spread and level the gravel, making the layer 1-2in(2.5-5cm) deep.

4 *If the soil under the gravel is good, you can plant straight into it. If it is poor, dig out a few extra trowelfuls and replace it with good-quality, soil-based potting mixture.*

5 *Make the planting hole a little larger than the plant pot. Knock the plant out and position the roots in the hole. Fill the gaps with more potting mixture and firm gently.*

7 *A small ornament completes the 'cameo'. Stone always looks well with gravel. This stone lantern has a Japanese feel about it, but a large rounded stone or a pile of smooth cobblestones would also work well.*

8 *The finished arrangement will be quite drought tolerant once the plants are established, but they will need regular watering until then.*

Juniperus x media
'Carberry Gold'

Euonymus
'Emerald 'n
Gold'

Thymus
'Archer's Gold',
a gold-leaved
thyme.

6 *A small group of plants makes more of a feature than a single one if space permits; choose plants that complement each other and that are reasonably drought tolerant.*

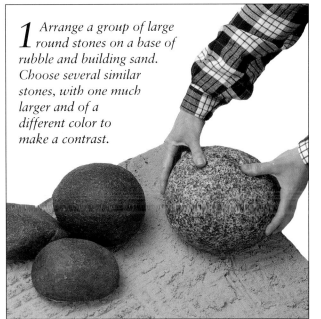

1 *Arrange a group of large round stones on a base of rubble and building sand. Choose several similar stones, with one much larger and of a different color to make a contrast.*

Using stones and gravel as a decorative feature

Here, large, rounded boulders and smaller cobbles are arranged together and drought-tolerant plants added to complement them. This scheme could add interest to a large area of gravel, such as a drive, but make sure you choose a spot where it does not interfere with pedestrians or car parking. Or try it within a patio, in a square where four paving slabs have been left out. Insert the plants through the hard foundation of the surrounding area of paving or gravel. Alternatively, leave a patch of bare soil to develop as a feature when laying the patio. If you do this, cover the soil with anti-weed mulch fabric (see page 24-25), insert the plants through it and cover it with gravel. A feature like this has a definite 'front' to it and should face the direction from which it is most often seen. If it is to be seen from all round, design it so that the largest stones and tallest 'key' plants are in the middle, with smaller groups and creeping plants radiating out in a roughly circular shape around them.

2 *Lay a patch of cobbles - smaller rounded stones, all the same color - onto the sand near the main group. Try adding a plant to the group between the biggest stones.*

Junipers are the most suitable conifers to grow in gravel; this one is 'Blue Star', which grows to only about 18x18in (45x45cm).

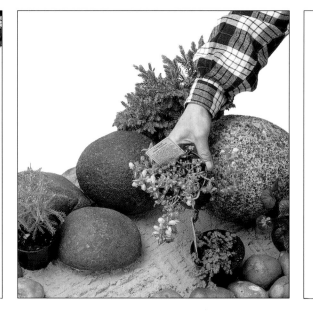

4 *Before planting, trowel out some of the sand and rubble to reach the soil beneath. Make a hole through the sand for each plant and add potting mixture. Remove the plants from their pots and insert them in place.*

3 *Choose drought-tolerant, smaller plants to put between the smaller stones. Stand them in place in their pots while you decide on the final planting arrangement.*

5 Finish off by spreading a layer of fine gravel between the stones and plants. Rounded stones look best and are smoother than crushed gravel, which has sharp edges. Use just enough to cover the sand.

6 After planting, water everything well in. Although the plants used here are fairly drought-tolerant, keep them watered until they are well established and can take care of themselves.

Cotton lavender is a dwarf evergreen shrublet with feathery silver foliage. It grows to about 24x24in (60x60cm).

Juniper 'Blue Star'

7 When the plants have grown up a bit, they will partly obscure the stones and look as if they grew there naturally. None will need pruning, although the cotton lavender can be trimmed lightly every spring or after flowering to keep it in shape.

Lamium 'Pink Pearls'

The gravel acts as a 'mulch', helping to retain moisture around the plant roots. It will need 'topping up' every year or two, as some sinks into the sand below.

Viola labradorica is happy in sun or shade, and spreads slowly by seeding itself into the gravel and gaps between stones.

Santolina incana (Cotton lavender)

Acaena glauca (A low-growing New Zealand burr)

27

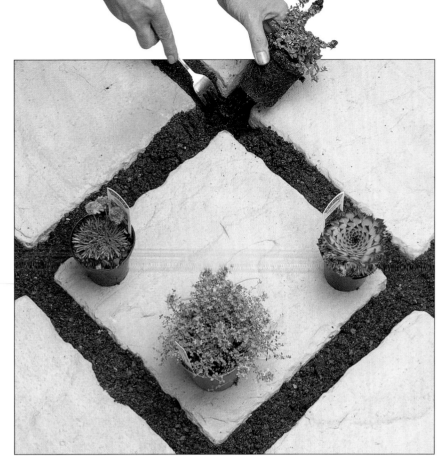

Planting in the cracks between slabs

Another way to add interest to a stretch of paving is to plant low-growing plants into the cracks. This is a good alternative to removing slabs and making beds (see pages 30-31) where space is short and you need a 'step-over' planting scheme. However, you could combine the two ideas and make a bigger and even more imaginative planting scheme. The best way to establish plants is to improve the soil and then plant or sow subjects that are suited to the conditions. If possible, improve the soil first before you lay the slabs, otherwise you will need to prise up the slabs around the cracks to work on the soil. Remove any rubble and stones and if the soil is very poor, replace some of it with good topsoil and a similar amount of well-rotted organic matter. Put any large plants in before replacing the slabs; be sure to lift the edges of the plants carefully out of the way to avoid damaging them when you replace the slabs. Alternatively, replace the slabs first and tuck smaller plants in between them. Use an old dinner fork or spoon to make planting holes in confined spaces.

Sowing seeds between slabs

Sprinkle seeds of alpine flowers, alyssum or creeping thymes thinly in the cracks between paving slabs. Do this instead of using grown plants or to fill the gaps between existing plants or for a denser planting scheme.

1 Choose a mixture of low, mound-forming plants and compact, low, spreading plants, particularly those with aromatic foliage. Plant them in the 'crossroads' between the slabs.

2 Plants in small pots are easier to fit into a limited space and are also cheaper to buy. After planting, firm the soil gently around each plant.

3 Arrange plants of contrasting shapes next to each other. Lift out the straggling ends of trailing plants onto the slabs when you plant them.

4 Make each planting hole about the same size as the rootball and pop the plant into place. Planting is much easier if you leave slightly wider gaps than usual between paving slabs.

5 Create groups by planting several adjacent corners. In time, the plants will almost cover those slabs, so remember to leave the main walking areas reasonably clear.

6 Sprinkle pea-sized shingle over the cracks and tuck it under creeping and rosette plants. This provides drainage around the necks and helps to prevent plants rotting.

Sempervivum
hybrid

Mother of thyme
(Thymus drucei
minus)

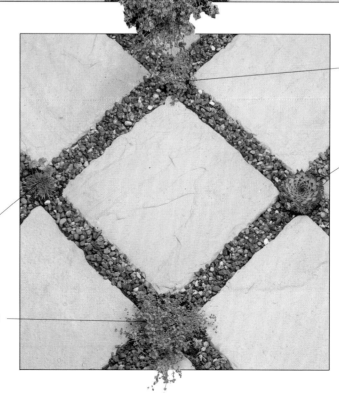

Thymus
'Doone Valley'

Miniature thrift
(Armeria
caespitosum)

7 Water plants and seeds in well and do not allow them to dry out during the first growing season. After that, they should be able to survive, except in unusually long, hot, dry spells.

29

Planting up beds in paving

One way of livening up a large area of paving is to make sunken beds by removing occasional slabs and planting in the spaces. If you are laying a new patio, it is simple to plan for such beds in advance. Instead of laying the usual rubble and concrete base over the whole area, leave the soil clear where your bed is to go. Improve the existing garden soil (assuming it is reasonably good) with organic matter, such as well-rotted garden compost, and pave round it. If you want to take up slabs from an existing paved area, chip away the cement from between the slabs and lever them out with a crowbar. If they are completely bedded into cement, you may not be able to avoid cracking them, and you may need a power hammer to remove them, together with the foundations beneath them, until you reach bare soil. Once the slabs are out, excavate as much rubble as you can from underneath and then refill with good topsoil, enriched with some extra organic matter. You could leave the bed 'flush' with the paving, or make a low raised edge to it using bricks or rope-edged tiles.

1 Decide where you want to create a bed and stand your plants, still in pots, on the slab you have decided to remove so you can judge the effect.

2 Prise the slab out - this one is easy as it is only loose-laid over soil. Excavate the hole so there is room to put in plenty of good soil for the plants.

3 If the existing soil is reasonably good, simply add some suitable organic matter to improve the texture and help moisture retention.

5 Planting compact rock plants in the corners 'ties in' the bed with rock plants growing in the cracks between other paving slabs nearby.

Saxifraga 'Beechwood White'

Sedum 'Lydium'

6 Plant all four corners for a neat, look. Choose plants that contrast in color and shape, and that will spill out over the surrounding paving.

4 Put the largest plant in the center of the new bed. This potentilla is compact and bushy, with a long flowering season through the summer.

Plants for paving

Because the surrounding slabs keep roots cool and prevent evaporation, the soil dries out much more slowly than potting mixture in containers. The plants have a bigger root run, too. The following plants will flourish in paving: Acaena, Alchemilla mollis, Cistus, Dianthus, Diascia, ericas, Frankenia, Helianthemum, junipers, rosemary, sedums, Sisyrinchium, thymes & sages.

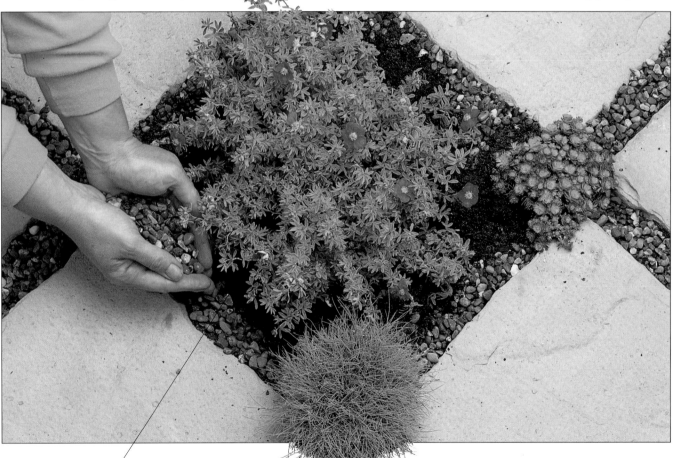

Potentilla fruticosa 'Red Robin'

Festuca glacialis

7 Tuck some gravel around and under the plants for decoration and drainage. Use the same gravel to cover gaps in the rest of the patio.

31

Ideas for plants and paving

Below: *You can remove the occasional paving slab in a patio and convert each area of exposed soil into a miniature bed. This is a good way of adding interest to a large expanse of paving or, as here, of fitting more plants into a 'busy' small patio.*

In odd backwaters of the garden, where nobody walks about much, you can plant flowers or rock plants into the cracks between paving. Drought-tolerant plants, including some kinds of rock plants, are the most suitable for a low-maintenance scheme (see page 31). But why not try something different? Self-sown seedlings of many kinds of hardy annuals are just as drought-tolerant. If the cracks are not cemented over and there is even the poorest soil between them, these plants often just 'arrive' without ever having been sown. The best way to get self-sown seedlings going is to plant suitable plants nearby - not in the patio itself - and let them set seed. Then simply pull up any that grow where you do not want them. Even tall plants like hollyhocks can look charming growing randomly in paving next to a wall, but for a more orderly look you may prefer to plant 'tamer' species into gaps or into small beds made by removing an occasional paving slab. In this case, be sure to improve the soil under the slabs, as grown plants are less accommodating than self-sown seedlings. Creeping plants with scented foliage are particularly pleasant. They contribute their lingering aroma to the air every time they are stepped on and lightly crushed - but do not walk on them too often. Non-flowering chamomile and creeping thymes are ideal. Try growing plants that spread over the paving, such as nasturtium, but choose a situation where they will not be walked on. And as a complete change, why not plant a small area with a herbal or alpine 'lawn' made of a mixture of low creeping plants, with stepping stones to allow you to pick your way through them?

Left: *Although it is an annual, alyssum will seed itself into cracks between paving, so there is often no need to keep replanting it every year. The flowers have a light honey scent.*

A mat of low-growing foliage plants makes a superb foil for taller flowering plants in this patio bed.

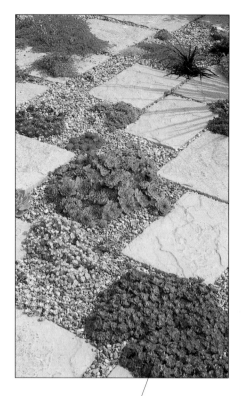

Left: *Heat- and drought-tolerant species of alpines are a good choice for planting between cracks in a hot sunny area; use pea shingle or gravel to topdress the soil between plants.*

Right: *Chamomile makes a delightful scented herbal ground covering. The variety 'Treneague' is best as it does not flower and remains compact in form. Use it around paved 'stepping stones' or in cracks between paving slabs, as it is not very hard wearing.*

The flowers are an attractive bonus on this variety of chamomile.

The dense leaf rosettes of houseleeks and similar plants suppress weeds between slabs.

Plants that self-seed in paving cracks

Flowering plants that develop from self-sown seedlings can create a delightfully casual, cottage garden look to any patio. The following plants will grow from seeds that germinate naturally: Alchemilla mollis, Alyssum, Antirrhinum *(Snapdragons),* Arabis, Calendula *marigolds,* Corydalis lutea *(Yellow corydalis),* Cymbalaria muralis *(Ivy-leaved toadflax),* Erinus alpinus, *Hollyhocks, Pansies and violas,* Viola labradorica, *Nasturtiums, and Wallflowers.*

Left: *You can make a small bed anywhere by lifting up several paving slabs, removing the foundation underneath and replacing it with topsoil. Use these beds to blunt the sharp edges of an angular feature. Here, a pebble-strewn bed softens the outline of a circular, brick-rimmed pond.*

Wooden decking

Decking made of hardwood to withstand the weather is another alternative patio surface. Raise up the decking so that air can circulate underneath to prevent rotting. It need only be a few inches above ground level, but you could create spectacular raised decks to give a view over the surrounding garden or countryside. Wooden decking looks particularly good in modern surroundings or teamed with a woodland or oriental-style garden. To make the most of the timber theme, use wooden containers and furniture on a deck, and choose plants that suit a timbered background. Camellias, miniature rhododendrons, hostas, hardy ferns and lilies in wooden tubs help create the feel of a woodland garden close to the house. For an ultramodern style, choose striking shapes like those of yucca, phormium and trachycarpus (Chusan palm), with plenty of exotic-looking half-hardy plants, such as agave, aeonium or abutilon. You could even add a gnarled log covered with airplants and other bromeliads. For an oriental feel, go for a few good, well-shaped, clipped conifers and bonsai shapes in oriental ceramic pots similar to large bonsai dishes - wider than they are high.

Above: Wood need not be used in a large area of decking. Here, a small 'cameo' patio area has been created in a secluded corner with wooden log 'tiles' laid in a bed of gravel.

Above: Here, wooden decking makes a natural background to many plants. The garden is full of moisture-loving subjects, while potted plants on the deck are drought-tolerant species.

Right: In this design, timber is the main feature and the understated planting scheme is based on green, gray and silvery foliage, with white, cream and purple/mauve flowers.

Preserving the wood

Decking is most suitable in a dry climate; in a damp environment the wood will soon become slippery, discolored and may rot. Cold, snowy winters will not harm the wood but it will suffer in mild, damp ones. Treat any timber exposed to the weather with a suitable preservative; some products contain natural colored stains that will restore and enhance its appearance. Lay wooden pieces as stepping stones on a free-draining base of rubble and gravel to delay rotting.

The dark blooms of pansies echo the rich wooden tones of the patio and complement the modern style of this container.

Right: An oriental-style garden with a natural background, clipped evergreen bushes, boulders and water, all overlooked from the deck of a timber house with overhanging eaves.

A water feature in a tub

Ponds are very popular garden features, but if you do not have space for a full-sized one, why not have a pond in a pot? They make good features for the patio, providing a succession of new attractions to enjoy - flowers, floating foliage, beautiful dragonflies and damselflies; even birds will come to drink. There are so many fascinating and lovely pond plants to grow that you will be spoilt for choice. In a very warm area, you could choose exotic tropical waterlilies, many of which have unusual blue flowers. Papyrus and sacred lotus both make large plants that would soon fill a tub on their own but look very stunning; these and tropical waterlilies should be moved to a slightly heated conservatory for the winter.

A wide range of aquatics will thrive in cooler areas. Choose a mixture of floating and upright marginal plants, including some with flowers and others with reedlike foliage. Good floating plants include water hyacinth (*Eichhornia crassipes*) and water chestnut (*Trapa natans*) - both of which need replacing each spring - frogbit (*Hydrocharis morsus-ranae*) and floating soldier (*Stratiotes aloides*), which looks like a half-submerged pineapple - best for a biggish barrel. If you want a waterlily, choose a pygmy variety as the rest grow too big and in any case need deeper water. For reedy shapes, go for dwarf reedmace, corkscrew rush (*Juncus effusus* 'Spiralis') or *Equisetum hyemale*, a domesticated horsetail.

5 Pygmy varieties of waterlily are suitable for a small 'pond' such as this. They need 6-9in (15-23cm) of water above their crowns.

4 This houttuynia is in a very small pot that barely needs to be submerged, so stand a brick on end to support it in the barrel.

1 As the water in the barrel will be too deep for many marginal pond plants, sink a few bricks around the edge to provide convenient planting shelves of different depths.

2 Sink the pots slowly into place, holding them while the potting mixture floods with water - this avoids the risk of soil washing out and clouding the water.

3 Most marginals need only 1-2in (2.5-5cm) of water above the top of their rootballs; adjust the bricks to provide the right water depth.

6 *Start new waterlilies off at a depth that allows their existing leaves to float comfortably on the surface of the water; lower them gradually later on.*

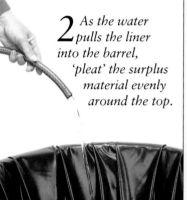

7 *The non-edible water chestnut (Trapa natans) is a floating water plant without any roots; just drop the plant gently into the water.*

8 *The finished 'potted pond' needs a site where it will get sun for at least half the day, but will not get too hot - one way to help is by standing other waterside plants in pots around the edge.*

Lining the barrel

1 *Drape a large square of flexible pond liner evenly over the barrel and allow the middle to drop down into the center.*

2 *As the water pulls the liner into the barrel, 'pleat' the surplus material evenly around the top.*

3 *Once the barrel is reasonably full, cut away any lining material that hangs more than 2-3in(5-7.5cm) over the edge.*

4 *Fold the overhang back once to make a firm edging strip. Secure it around the rim of the barrel with waterproof tape.*

Dwarf reedmace or miniature bulrush (Typha minima)

Lobelia 'Queen Victoria'

Houttuynia cordata 'Chameleon'

Water chestnut (Trapa natans)

Pygmy waterlily (Nymphaea pygmaea 'Rubra')

Mimulus *hybrid*

Small water features

Small water features add movement, sounds and interest to a patio. They are usually cheaper and easier to install than a large feature and less work to maintain. If small children visit the garden, you may prefer not to have standing water; a fountain or millstone feature is far safer. Submersible pumps can turn terracotta jars and other containers into the source of a stream, which can flow into a gravel bed to be recirculated back again. A tiny raised pond in a half barrel looks good, surrounded by plants in containers, with a few floating plants or a miniature waterlily inside. Or use an old sink, raised up on blocks and disguised by evergreens. You could do away with water entirely by making a contained bog garden in a large container or bed to grow compact, moisture-loving plants, such as hostas, astilbes and hardy ferns. Or make a dry riverbed - a winding narrow sunken bed of gravel with various sized cobbles set into it, with occasional outcrops of iris and other typical waterside plants to set the scene. This looks particularly effective in a small courtyard garden.

Dappled shade adds to the charm of this group of patio containers

Above: *A potted water garden in ceramic pots; four are planted with miniature waterlilies and floating or marginal water plants. The rest house ferns, lilies and iris.*

Choosing waterlilies

Miniature waterlilies for tiny features need 6-9in(15-23cm) of water above their crowns. Choose from Nymphaea pygmaea 'Alba' (double white), N. laydekeri 'Purpurea' (double maroon-red), and N. pygmaea 'Helvola' (double pale yellow). Leave them planted in the net pots you buy them in. Every 2-3 years divide them in spring and repot the best piece into ordinary garden soil with no fertilizer.

'Froebeli' needs 6-12in(15-30cm) of water above the crown.

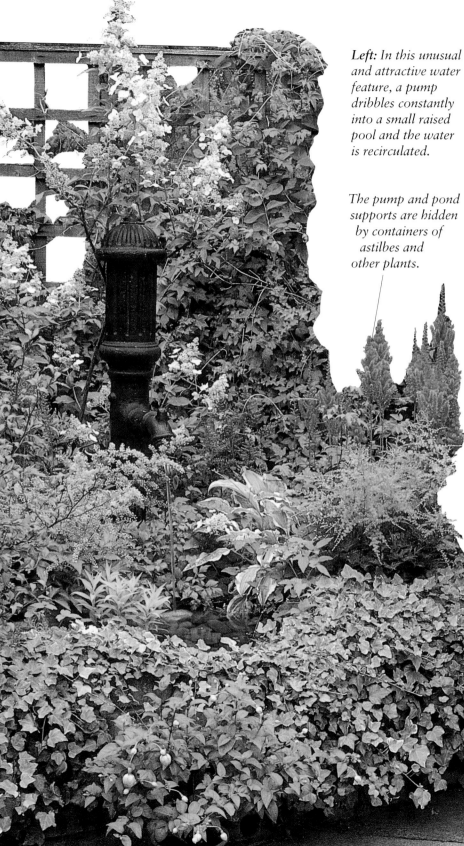

Left: In this unusual and attractive water feature, a pump dribbles constantly into a small raised pool and the water is recirculated.

The pump and pond supports are hidden by containers of astilbes and other plants.

Left: Here, water squirts from a jet into a terracotta pot and overflows onto the pebbles. Water is recirculated from here back via the pot. There is all the sound and sparkle of running water, but it is quite safe for children.

Below: The pump for this tiny feature is hidden under the stones in the pot. It 'draws together' the paving stones and various foliage shapes and sizes around it to make a charismatic cameo in a corner of the patio.

The water emerges through the largest of the pebbles in the arrangement.

Larger water features

A water feature need not just be a small decorative feature on a patio; it can be the main attraction. The patio can be designed entirely around the pond. If you opt for this sort of style, the usual annuals and hanging baskets rarely look right. Keep to a water garden theme throughout. Use water plants in sunken bog garden beds lined with plastic or butyl rubber, or grow them in large, water-filled containers nearby. You can also use moisture-loving herbaceous plants, ferns, wildflowers and native shrubs to continue the natural look. These are best planted in beds rather than pots, as they tend to be too tall and top heavy for pots and in any case must not dry out. Instead of colorful synthetic patio slabs, choose natural stone and gravel, or timber, log slices and bark chippings for hard surfacing. Pick patio furniture with a natural look, too - stone benches or wooden tables and chairs will look far more at home than highly colored, modern upholstered seats. Water always attracts wildlife, so plan your pond so that birds can get down to the edge to bathe and drink - shelving sides also permit hedgehogs to get out if they fall in.

Place water plants into special plastic baskets lined with hessian, taking care not to damage the roots. Top up with pea shingle to prevent the soil floating away once they are submerged. The plant being potted up here is Houttuynia cordata *'Chameleon', which is grown mainly for its attractive foliage.*

Below: *The upright leaves of the variegated water iris (Iris laevigata 'Variegata') accentuate the shape of this fountain in a small formal pool. The water iris will do best in shallow water and a warm sunny spot.*

Left: *In shady corners, a fountain adds sparkle and sounds to highlight a garden planted with ferns and foliage. Arum lily flowers and variegated hosta leaves help to create a cool, green-and-white color scheme.*

Above: *Pebbles are a great way of hiding the liner of a water feature; here the shallow sloping sides have been banked up with more pebbles to create reflections and also a watering place for birds and other wildlife.*

Iris pseudacorus *cultivar*

Iris laevigata *cultivar*

Iris sibirica *cultivar*

The huge leaves of Gunnera manicata

The tall blue flowers of Iris sibirica

The pink plumes of Astilbe arendsii *cultivar*

The yellow blooms of globe flowers (Trollius hybridus)

Left: *Here, a bog garden for moisture-loving plants has been constructed alongside a pond, but separate from it. This prevents mud from the bog garden making the pond water dirty.*

41

Walls and raised beds

The best way to make good use of the limited space on a patio is by gardening in three dimensions: on the ground, up walls and in raised beds. This allows you to get in more plants and to see and enjoy them better. Each 'tier' will be seen against a proper background, and each plant will have space of its own without being overcrowded. On a patio, the tallest plants will be those growing on walls, and the next tier can be flowering subjects in wall or hanging baskets. Somewhat below them - anything from 12-18in(30-45cm) to just below waist height - raised beds add another layer of color. These may be around the edge of the patio or inside it as a walk-round bed. Containers on the ground add yet another level of color and their flowers will stand out well against the brick or stone sides of the raised beds. Finally, let into the patio surface, are sunken beds or plants growing in cracks between paving. By using this simple multistory technique, and choosing suitable plants, you can pack the tiniest patio with interesting detail and a changing spectrum of colors all year.

Below: Raised beds around a patio do not dry out as quickly as containers because they hold more soil. For a really labor-saving scheme, avoid annuals and grow perennials instead.

Easier gardening

Raised beds enable people with physical handicaps to garden, as they can do so without bending, and even from a wheelchair. Pave the ground around the bed with a level, nonslip surface and allow enough room around the edge for easy access. Make beds narrow enough so the middle can be reached without bending over, and at just below waist height - slightly lower for wheelchairs. For the visually impaired, include scented plants and those with felty leaves that are pleasant to touch.

Left: *It is not unnatural for plants to grow in tiers like this. In the wild, layers of vegetation have specialized to take advantage of the conditions at different levels. In the garden it is a good idea to keep the background colors the same to show off a riotous mixture of plants to best effect.*

Right: *Enliven a large area of walling by creating recesses in it that are large enough to hold small containers. Planted with trailing plants, such as lobelia, the effect can be stunning.*

An assortment of foliage and flowering plants provide a mellow display that can be changed with the seasons.

The colors of the lobelias harmonize with the pinkish tones of this sandstone wall.

These wooden raised beds blend in with the bricks used for the patio surface and echo the warm tones of the terracotta containers.

Right: *A free-standing raised bed adds easy-care color and a change of level to flat paving. Prettily planted and with seats around the edge, it can form the focal point of a patio.*

Creating a small hanging basket

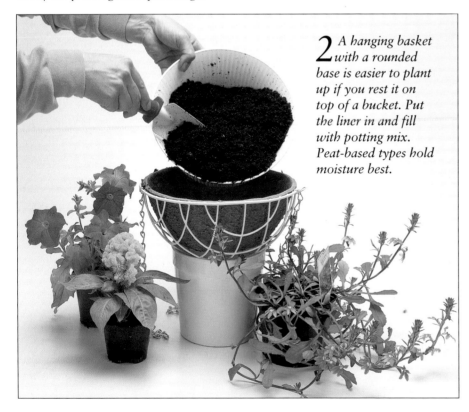

This attractive spreading plant is ideal to form the core of the arrangement.

1 *This traditional wire basket has a rigid liner made of recycled compressed paper. Three plants are enough to fill this small basket, as one of the plants grows quite large.*

2 *A hanging basket with a rounded base is easier to plant up if you rest it on top of a bucket. Put the liner in and fill with potting mix. Peat-based types hold moisture best.*

You do not have to plant up large, extravagant, multicolored hanging basket schemes. Those planned around a single color can be very effective, too. What is more, they look cool and sophisticated. On a patio, color-themed container schemes can be designed to coordinate with patio furniture, such as awnings and cushion covers, or perhaps the curtains around the patio doors. But putting together a planting scheme that uses only a few colors is not nearly as easy as working with the full spectrum. It can easily end up looking rather dull - unless you borrow some of the 'tricks of the trade' used by garden designers working on full-sized, color-themed gardens. The secret of success is to make maximum use of contrasting shapes and textures. Seek out plants whose flowers are the same color, but different in shape and size. Where possible, choose plants with silvery gray or felty leaves as a change from plain green. Look for foliage with different sizes and textures, too. Use some large, leathery leaves and some small, airy leaves like those of ferns. And even if you are planning a single color for your theme, do try to bring in touches of a second color, even if it is not particularly noticeable. It is this that gives the whole arrangement depth, as the effect is one of shading. The famous white garden at Sissinghurst in southern England, for example, is not entirely white. It contains subtle hints of mauve, with silver, gray and variegated foliage. However, it is notoriously difficult to achieve total success with a white garden; red and orange, yellow, or blue and purple are much easier to work with.

An easier way to create a color scheme is to introduce a totally contrasting color, but in very small amounts. In nature, many flowers have a different colored 'eye' in the center. This would be a good second color to use for a natural highlight, perhaps in the middle of the arrangement. Color schemes are fun to play around with. Try out several ideas by standing the plants together before committing yourself to planting them.

3 *Plant trailing or sprawling plants at the front of the basket. Turn the plant round so that it naturally leans over the edge and soon makes a good display.*

4 *The other plants in this display pick out the two colors, blue and yellow, in the flowers of the large sprawling plant that forms the centerpiece.*

5 *The trailing plant should scramble around the other two without smothering them. Plant them against the back edge of the basket. They should be a little taller than the trailer, but not over-dominant.*

Creating a small hanging basket

7 *Gather the chains up - in this model, the chains can be detached from the hanging hook for ease of planting - and hang the arrangement in a sheltered, sunny spot, so that the trailing plant faces to the front.*

Petunia

Cockscomb
(Celosia cristata)

Scaevola aemula

6 *Water the plants well in, making sure the soil is evenly moist. A rigid liner holds water a little better than a traditional moss-lined one, but it still needs watering daily in warm weather.*

1 *This flexible 'whalehide' liner is made up of overlapping panels that adjust to different models of hanging basket of the same width. The white fiber circle helps to retain water.*

A mixed hanging basket

Summer bedding plants are the traditional favorites for hanging baskets, but some of the more vigorous, trailing or sprawling summer-flowering rock plants are good choices, too, because they enjoy sun and good drainage. In fact, the free-draining environment of a hanging basket suits them better than it does many bedding plants, as rock plants recover sooner from the occasional water shortage. Choose species that flower over most of the summer. Although they are not as well known as bedding plants, many are available in garden centers, including *Diascia cordifolia, Convolvulus cneorum, Helianthemum* (rock rose), *Leucanthemum hosmariense*, miniature geranium species, such as *G. lancastriense*, and some of the campanulas, such as *C. carpatica, C. portenschlagiana* and *C. isophylla*. You can grow a mixture of suitable rock plants on their own, or mix them with other naturally drought-resistant plants, such as herbs. Or mix them with traditional bedding plants for a striking but unusual combination. Although most rock plants are perfectly hardy, it is not a good idea to leave them in a hanging basket for the winter. Remove them when you clear away the old bedding plants in the fall. Cut the rock plants back to within about 4in(10cm) of their base to tidy them up and then pot them into soil-based potting mix in pots just large enough to hold their roots. Keep them in a cold greenhouse, cold frame or in a sheltered part of the garden protected from excess damp. Reuse the same plants in new planting schemes in hanging baskets or other containers the following year. You can also propagate them by taking cuttings in spring. The young plants will be ready to plant up in about eight weeks.

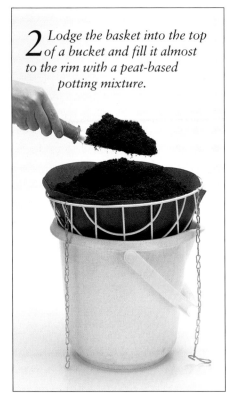

2 *Lodge the basket into the top of a bucket and fill it almost to the rim with a peat-based potting mixture.*

3 *Before planting, cut the top from a plastic bottle and sink it into the center of the basket. The 'funnel' makes watering easier.*

4 *A mixture of trailing and floppy sprawling plants will create a soft sphere of color all round the basket. This compensates for the fact that only the top of the basket will be planted up.*

5 Plant the taller plants in the middle of the basket, forming a ring around the funnel to hide it. They will also give the arrangement a definite center.

Campanula carpatica

Petunia

Petunia

Diascia 'Ruby Field'

Lobelia

The dark liner provides a good background.

8 Hang the basket in a warm, sheltered spot where it will get direct sun for at least half the day, but ideally more. Give the basket a quarter turn every week.

6 Add tumbling and trailing plants around the sides of the basket to conceal the edge. Turn them round so that their stems - which usually trail mostly in one direction - cascade over the edges to give an instant effect.

7 The finished basket already has a mature look about it. Water it well so that the potting mixture holds as much moisture as it can, then fill the plastic funnel 'reservoir' in the center of the basket. Refill it every day.

A classic hanging basket

Hanging baskets are one of the most popular containers for patios. They are often available in early summer already planted up, in full flower, and ready to hang up. This is very convenient if you want an instant display, but buying 'off the peg' is the most expensive way of getting a good hanging basket. It is much cheaper - and certainly more creative - to buy your own empty basket and plant it up yourself. You can reuse the same basket every year, and they are available in a wide range of shapes, sizes and styles, made from either plastic or wire, with solid or open sides. Open-sided baskets need lining with either moss or one of the proprietary basket liners available in garden centers.

The best time to plant a hanging basket is early summer, after the frosts. However, if you have a frost-free greenhouse or sunroom to keep it in for a while, you can plant it in late spring and keep it under cover until the weather is warm enough to put it outside. ('Harden' the plants off first by putting the basket out on fine days and then bringing it in at night for the first week or two.) Summer bedding are the most popular plants for hanging baskets. Traditional favorites include trailing plants, such as petunias, ivy-leaved pelargoniums, fuchsia teamed with lobelia, and compact, upright plants, such as busy lizzie, tuberous begonias and zonal pelargoniums. These plants will flower through the summer.

4 *Now tuck a few larger plants through the sides of the basket. Push the roots through from outside so they reach well into the soil and rest on the ledge of moss.*

3 *Place more moss inside the basket, about halfway up the sides. The lobelia roots must remain in the center of the basket, surrounded by soil, not moss.*

1 *For a traditional moss-lined wire basket, start by placing some thick wads of moss, green side down, in the base of the basket. Soak the moss first so it is easier to work with.*

2 *Tuck trailing lobelia plants through the edge of the basket's base, with their roots resting on the moss. Space the plants out evenly all round for a symmetrical display.*

5 *This shows how the moss is used with its dirty underside uppermost. It takes up water better this way and the green top is then visible around the outside.*

6 *Complete the mossing of the sides, taking the moss slightly above the rim of the basket to retain the soil. Fill with a peat-based potting mixture.*

Pelargonium 'Coco Rico'

Busy lizzie (Impatiens)

9 *The finished basket illustrates a traditional spherical planting scheme. As the plants grow, the basket will completely disappear beneath a mass of flowers.*

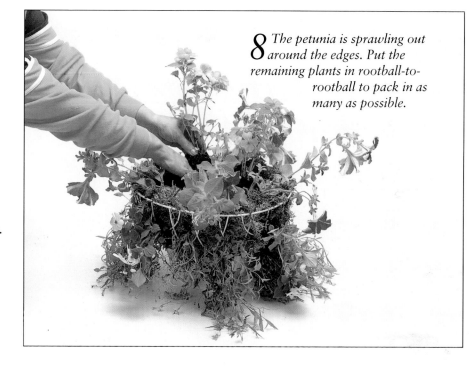

Fuchsia

Petunia 'Express Red Star'

Busy lizzie (Impatiens)

Lobelia 'Blue Fountain'

7 *Plant the top of the basket from the center outwards to avoid damaging the plants. Turn the basket round as you work. Put the tallest plants in the center for best effect.*

Once planted, allow the petunia stems to splay out.

The lobelias will soon cover the sides.

8 *The petunia is sprawling out around the edges. Put the remaining plants in rootball-to-rootball to pack in as many as possible.*

49

Hanging baskets for a patio display

There are a few 'tricks of the trade' to creating eye-catching hanging baskets. Plant as early as you can, so that the baskets have time to mature before you hang them up - newly planted baskets never look their best until the plants have filled out a bit. If you have a frost-free greenhouse or sunroom, plant baskets in late spring and keep them under cover until the last risk of frost is past, before putting them out. 'Harden' off the plants for two weeks by putting them outside during the day and bringing them back indoors at night, before leaving them out altogether. Otherwise, plant baskets up as soon as the last frost in your area is past in early summer, and really pack the plants in; baskets look best when slightly over - rather than under-filled. Where possible, plant the sides as well as the top of the basket for a fuller display. Choose plants that are already in bud or with flowers just open, for an instant result. Caring for hanging baskets is not difficult, but they do need a little time every day. Feed and water them regularly; baskets soon suffer and are much harder to restore to good condition than to keep that way in the first place. In a sunny spot, hanging baskets may need watering once or even twice daily in summer. Check the soil with your fingers, and water it before it is completely dry. Cut off dead flowerheads regularly; they not only look untidy, but also stop plants producing new flowers, because they are concentrating on setting seed instead.

Left: One advantage of hanging baskets is that you can move them around the garden, where and whenever they are needed to give instant, portable color. Here, pendulous begonias brighten up an arch while the climbers are not in flower.

Below: A special place alongside a front door deserves a really spectacular basket, such as this one, which is planted with Helichrysum, pelargoniums, single tagetes and some trailing plectranthus.

Above: Baskets planted entirely with the same kind of plant can look very spectacular, too. Here, the blue lobelias in the baskets were chosen to match the blue-and-white color scheme of the patio in general.

Above: To make the most of a really stunning basket, display it inside a 'frame' - an arch, alcove or in front of a doorway, as here. A darker, neutral-colored or contrasting background enhances the display even further.

Left: A basket of herbs not only looks decorative, it also provides delicious scents. Here nasturtiums (which have edible flowers) are combined with variegated pineapple mint and a silvery curry plant to good effect.

Silver and silver variegated plants

Cotton lavender (Santolina incana). Variegated mind your own business (Helxine soleirolii 'Argentea'). Nasturtium 'Alaska'. Silver feather (Pyrethrum ptarmicaeflorum). Helichrysum petiolatum. Fuchsia 'Sunray'. Dusty miller (Cineraria bicolor). Ballota pseudodictamnus. Variegated ivies. Variegated hop (Humulus japonicus 'Variegatus'). Ipomoea 'Spice Islands Mixed'. Thymus 'Silver Posie'. Pineapple mint.

A vivid wall basket to take the eye

1 *This type of wall basket is designed for use indoors or out; for outdoor use, first make holes in the base. Tap through the weak points marked on the base with the tip of a screwdriver.*

2 *Half fill the basket with a peat-based potting mix that will retain moisture in such a small, densely planted container. Set out your plants.*

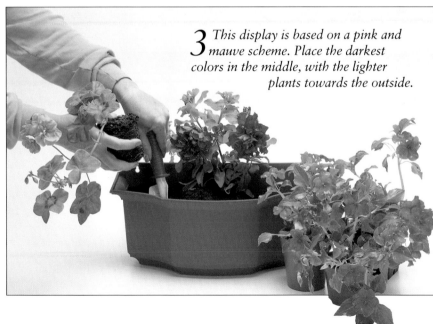

3 *This display is based on a pink and mauve scheme. Place the darkest colors in the middle, with the lighter plants towards the outside.*

Large expanses of wall look very much more interesting when they are decorated with containers of colorful flowers, and as an alternative to normal hanging baskets, you can also buy wall baskets. These are like hanging baskets that have been sliced in half and mounted on a wall. Wall baskets are useful where there is not enough room for normal hanging baskets, or where a container mounted flush against the wall looks better. They are also a useful way of adding interest to a fence or the side of a shed. You can also hang wall baskets from trellis with hooks, or mount them more permanently on a wall. A single wall basket can look rather lonely on a large wall, so group several together for a better display. Threes or fives always look better than even numbers, and a staggered row looks better than a straight line. A single wall basket tends to look best where there is less room, perhaps on a short piece of wall, or filling a gap between climbers.

From a practical point of view, be prepared for wall baskets to need more watering than normal hanging baskets. Due to the relatively small volume of soil they contain, they will also need frequent feeding to keep the plants in them looking their best for the entire growing season. The key to a good wall basket is matching the plants to the location. Walls are often in shade for much of the day. In this case, plants such as mimulus, busy lizzie, ivies, fuchsias, *Begonia semperflorens* and campanulas are the best choice. Provided they are already in flower when you plant them, they will carry on quite happily. In a hot sunny spot, it is best to go for real sun-lovers; mesembryanthemum, lampranthus, echeveria, portulaca and other succulent plants are naturally drought-proof. Herbs, too, are a good choice for wall baskets in sunny positions; they look particularly good in terracotta containers. But for a position that gets sun for about half the day, the usual range of summer-flowering annuals - the same sort of thing you would plant in a hanging basket - are ideal.

4 Knock the plants out of their pots and plant the rootballs as closely together as possible. The more plants you can pack into the container, the better it will eventually look.

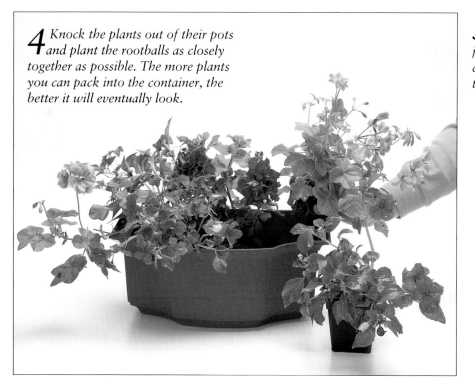

5 If you can spot even the tiniest gap, see if you can make room for just one more plant. Put plants of different colors next to each other, so that each one stands out.

Purple flowers fade to grayish purple

Petunia 'Purple Pirouette'

Ivy-leaved pelargonium 'Butterfly'

6 Water the finished basket very well after planting. Expect the soil to dry out very quickly, so check it twice daily. Wall planters can dry out even faster than hanging baskets.

Impatiens 'Accent Lilac'

Ivy-leaved pelargonium 'Summer Showers'

7 Tease out the trailing stems of ivy-leaved geraniums, so that they hang over the front of the planter. Hang the wall basket in its final position, in a sheltered, sunny spot.

1 The pot will be quite heavy once it is filled with potting mixture, so place it in its final position before you fill and plant it. Put 1in(2.5cm) of gravel in the base for drainage.

2 Add a little soil-based potting mix. Plant clematis deeply to keep their roots cool and to help them recover from clematis wilt, should they be affected by it.

3 Plant the clematis so that the base rests on the soil above the gravel drainage layer and the top of the rootball is 3in(7.5cm) below the rim of the tub.

Planting a clematis in a patio container

Climbers are always useful round a patio, which traditionally is surrounded on two or three sides by walls. House walls and ornamental block walls built to add privacy all benefit from the softening effect of climbers. But on a patio it can be a problem finding somewhere to plant them if the ground is covered by paving or concrete. The simple answer is to plant climbers in containers. Naturally, you will need a reasonably large container for each plant. Half barrels or tubs measuring 15-18in(38-45cm) in diameter are ideal. But the most important thing is to choose the right kind of climber. Very vigorous ones, such as Russian vine, wisteria, Virginia creeper and large species clematis, such as *Clematis montana*, are not suitable. Climbing roses do not like being confined in containers, so avoid them, too. However, suitable climbers include passionflower, purple grape vine (*Vitis vinifera* 'Purpurea'), and the unusual but very pretty *Ampelopsis brevipedunculata* 'Elegans', which has tricolor variegated foliage in pink, cream and green. Hybrid clematis, widely celebrated as superb garden climbers, are hugely underrated as container plants. (These are the popular kinds with large, wide-open flowers, such as 'Nelly Moser'.) A single climber looks good on its own, but on a large wall why not group three containers together? Plant one with a colored leaf climber, such as the purple-leaved grape, and the other two with clematis that flower at different times, for a pretty effect that lasts all summer.

All climbers in containers need generous watering and frequent feeding. Use any good-quality general-purpose liquid feed, correctly diluted, once or twice a week from spring to midsummer. In spring, give clematis a dose of liquid tomato feed, as they benefit from the extra potash. Clematis that need hard pruning to within a few inches of the soil each year are the most suitable for containers. They are easy to repot into fresh soil when they need it, every three years in spring.

Clematis 'Niobe'. This dependable variety will produce single flowers throughout the summer months and can grow up to 10ft(3m) high.

4 *Trowel more potting mixture into the corners of the container and firm it down gently around the rootball. Fill the tub to within 1in (2.5cm) of the rim with potting mix.*

7 *Spread out a couple of handfuls of bark chippings or similar water-retentive mulch to keep the soil cool and moist.*

5 *Secure the clematis cane to the trellis with a plant tie. You could untie the climber from its cane and retie it to the trellis if it were not in flower and likely to be damaged.*

6 *Spread out the new shoots growing from the top of the clematis, above the point where it is tied to its cane, and spread them out over the trellis. Tie loosely in place.*

8 *Water the plant in well and there you have it - an instant climber in full bloom! Cut this variety down to just above soil level in early spring.*

Trellis on the patio

All sorts of interesting effects can be achieved using trellis. Often it is secured to a wall to support climbers or wall shrubs and is easy to remove if you need to maintain or paint the wall. Trellis can also make a screen around a patio for instant privacy and then you can grow climbers on it, either planted in a bed in the ground, or in tubs or troughs on the paving in front of it. Or you can suspend wall baskets and other hanging containers from it. Trellis can be bolted to a timber structure or combined with pergola poles to make an enclosed corner, a shaded area for bonsai trees or woodland plants, or a romantic arbor covered with roses. Traditional trellis has a diamond lattice pattern, but it is also available in a range of other styles, including panels that 'concertina' and stretch to fit various shapes. Trellis is best used in reasonably sheltered places. Only the strongest kinds can withstand frequent gale force winds, so make sure that supporting timbers are strong and well fixed, and clear away displays of baskets and annual climbers before the winter.

Left: *A modern version of the arbor - an enclosed seating area that is quick and easy to erect. The slatted sides provide privacy and shelter, and make a home for plants in wall baskets.*

Above: *Plants thrive in the shelter of a pergola. The climbers growing up the trellis screen at the back will be able to grow out along the poles to complete the effect.*

Right: A trellis screen is the ideal place to display a collection of wall baskets. Here, all sorts of different plants and containers have been used to create a random and colorful display.

Plastic and wire half baskets are easy to hook onto trellis. And there are plenty of supports available to hang up single pots.

Below: Wall-trained shrubs, such as this pyracantha, need a means of support. Trellis provides an attractive background with plenty of places to tie shoots to keep the plant looking tidy.

Climbers for the patio

With walls on one or more sides, a patio is the natural place to grow climbers. They soften the hard appearance of walls, and help the architecture to blend into the surrounding garden. Jasmine, honeysuckle and clematis are all good choices, but avoid prickly plants such as roses. For a Mediterranean look, try luscious grapes, figs or peaches. (Naturally dwarf peach trees are available for growing in pots under the name 'patio peaches'.) For colorful foliage, grow the purple-leaved grape *Vitis vinifera* 'Purpurea', which has small, sweet, purple grapes, and *Ampelopsis brevipendunculata* 'Elegans', which has tricolor variegated leaves - both associate particularly well with clematis. For an exotic tropical look, go for spectacularly perfumed or large, colorful climbers, which are often slightly tender, such as passionflower. Do not, however, grow climbers intended for a conservatory (such as bougainvillea) outside unless you live in a Mediterranean climate. Climbers normally need a sheltered spot that gets plenty of sun. Ivy and climbing hydrangea are self-supporting, holding themselves onto the wall with clinging 'suckers' or aerial roots that push into tiny crevices. Be cautious about growing these on the house, but on screen walls they can do no harm. Most climbers need to be supported - fix wall nails or trellis to the wall to tie in their stems.

Above: Clematis 'Ville de Lyon' *flowers continuously from summer until the fall and grows up to 12ft (3.7m) in height. For a vigorous and colorful display every year, prune this climber back to a few inches above ground level in early spring.*

Left: Trumpet vine, Campsis tagliabuana *'Madame Galen', is a vigorous climber with huge sprays of exotic trumpet flowers in summer, but it must have a warm, sheltered and very sunny spot in the garden to do well.*

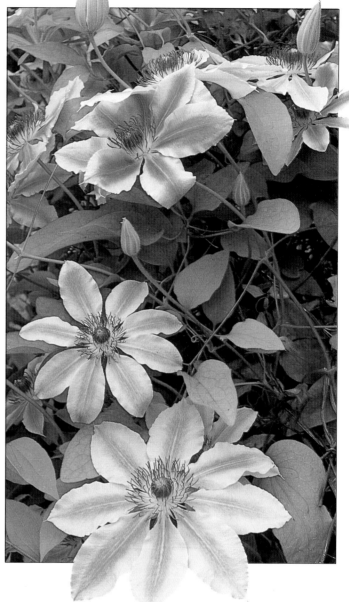

Unusual climbers

Trachelospermum asiaticum
(slightly tender)
Rosa banksiae lutea *(Banksian
rose, slightly tender)*
Solanum crispum *(Chilean
potato tree, fairly hardy)*
Clianthus puniceus *(Parrots bill,
rather tender)*
Jasminum x stephanense *(hardy)*
Akebia quinata *(unusual flowers,
good foliage)*
Cytisus battandieri *(Pineapple
broom, wall shrub)*
Actinidia kolomikta *(leaves with
pink and cream variegated tips)*

Left: *There are many varieties of
passionflower, but not all are hardy
outdoors. This hybrid,* Passiflora x
caeruleo-racemosa, *will grow on a
sunny wall. Prune hard in spring.*

Above: *Clematis 'Nelly Moser' is an
old favorite. Grow it on a wall that
does not receive the strong midday
sun, as the beautifully marked flowers
quickly fade. No pruning is needed.*

Left: Actinidia kolomikta *and Clematis
'Hagley Hybrid' scramble through
each other to make an interesting
combination. The magenta flower is*
Geranium psilostemon.

Containers on patios

Containers are to patios what pot plants are to living rooms. And just like pot plants indoors, patio containers can be replanted, replaced or rearranged whenever you like. They are the final touches that complete the exterior decorating scheme. The containers themselves can match the surrounding furnishings and fittings or relate more to the plants in them. The most popular and successful plants for containers are naturally compact, heat- and sun loving, and provide color and interest over the longest possible season. Annual bedding plants are traditional favorites, but 'all-year-round' shrubs and herbaceous plants are growing in favor. The way containers of plants are displayed can make a huge difference to the look of a patio. A single, well-grown plant, beautifully displayed against a good background and with its own well defined space round it, can look stunning. Pick up tips by studying flower arranging, looking at displays in shop windows and the pictures in this book - and then have fun trying out some of your own ideas.

Above: Another way of turning a collection of plants into a unified display is to grow them in similar containers and group them together in a space of their own. This helps them stand out from their background, too.

Left: Banking containers up on staging or upturned pots makes more of a display - here ornamental cabbage and pot chrysanthemums are growing in terracotta pots, some of which have been roughly marbled with green paint.

Container ideas

Containers can be used all year round; in winter, polyanthus and winter-flowering heathers with evergreens, such as ivies, make a welcoming sight (right). Group containers together and link them with a theme, however minor. You could include one plant of the same color in every group around the patio. Or use a plant of the same kind - perhaps a pelargonium - in each group. Or use the same style of container for all the plants. Try out different backgrounds, too.

Variegated-leaved pelargoniums

Pelargoniums

Golden bay

Above: *All sorts of tender, exotic plants can stand outside on a warm, sunny patio in summer to add to the subtropical feeling. Citrus plants, with their scented flowers, are specially delightful.*

Begonia semperflorens

Begonia semperflorens

Pineapple flower (Eucomis bicolor)

Livingstone daisies (Mesembryathemum)

Trailing lobelias

Variegated nasturtium (Tropaeolum nanum 'Alaska Mixed')

Echeverias and sempervivums

Californian poppy

Right: *A sunken patio or one surrounded by low walls creates an intimate feeling, and helps trap the heat. Grow sunloving plants in them, such as those shown here.*

Heathers and conifers

The heather cultivars being used here need ericaceous potting mix, which the conifers will not mind.

Nowadays, many people look for easy-care but stunning all-year-round patio displays. Evergreen plants are the basis of this type of scheme. They look good all the time, but need minimum maintenance. One of the most interesting ideas is a mixed planting scheme, which is almost a miniature garden in a tub. Some of the most suitable subjects include dwarf conifers, heathers and grassy plants. You could also add very compact evergreen shrubs, such as variegated euonymus, for variety and tuck in a few small spring bulbs or alpines for seasonal interest. One point to watch when planning this type of scheme is growth rates. A large mixed tub can soon look unbalanced if some subjects 'take over', so always check how big and how fast you can expect everything to grow. Check, too, for soil requirements. Many heathers, for example, must have a lime-free potting mix. Conifers and many evergreen shrubs will be happy in this, too, but some evergreen shrubs, such as box, prefer normal soil, so do not plant them in the same container.

1 Select the heathers and a couple of dwarf conifers - an upright and a domed variety will look good.

2 Fill the tub with potting mix to within a pot's depth of the top and stand the plants in it while you arrange them. The tall upright conifer will look best towards the back of the display.

3 Tap the plants out of their pots and put them as close together as possible, so that the tub is well filled and looks instantly mature. Variegated evergreens add more interest.

4 *Distribute the flowering heathers throughout the arrangement, intermingling them with the different colored foliage of the other plants.*

Notice how the contrasting shapes enhance the display.

5 *When everything has been planted, tuck a few handfuls of bark chippings in between the plants to give them a pleasing background that goes well with the wooden tub. It also acts as a moisture-retaining mulch.*

Evergreens in tubs

Variations on the evergreen theme include gold-leaved and variegated evergreen plants. Grow the larger varieties as specimens in individual tubs. In a shady garden, try evergreen ferns and variegated ivies. Box grows in shade, as long as it gets at least two hours of sun every day - a potted topiary tree would make quite a novelty.

Every two to three years, repot the whole display into new soil. Alternatively, scrape away the top 2in(5cm) of soil between the plants and replace it each spring. Deadhead occasionally, but feed and water regularly.

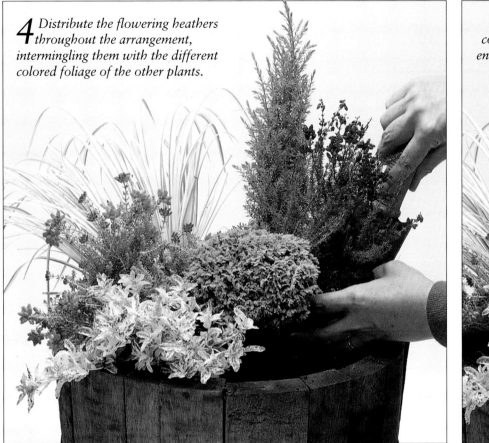

Erica tetralix 'Pink Star'

Acorus gramineus 'Ogon'

Juniperus communis 'Compressa'

Chamaecyparis thyoides 'Ericoides'

Erica cinerea 'Katinka'

Erica vagans 'St Keverne'

Euonymus fortunei 'Harlequin'

6 *The finished arrangement should last for several years before the plants get too big and need replacing. Clip back heathers after flowering and water in dry spells, even in winter. Evergreens can go brown if they dry out.*

The patio in spring

Even though it may be too cold to sit outside in spring, the patio is still visible from indoors and a colorful display of flowers is specially welcome at the end of a long winter. Good plants for spring displays include bulbs - daffodils, hyacinths, tulips, etc - and flowers such as polyanthus, wallflowers, forget-me-nots, stocks and double bellis daisies. In mild areas, you can plant these out in the fall after removing the summer annuals. However, by waiting until spring, you may find a wider range of plants available and as they have not had to weather the winter outside, they will probably be in better shape than those planted out in the fall. Harden them off in a cold frame or start off by standing them outside during the day and bringing them in at night for a week or so before planting. Choose plants that are still in tight bud rather than those with wide open flower, to give them a bit of time to adjust to the conditions before the flower opens. Add a few evergreens, such as ivies and small conifers, as temporary background plants to set off a container of flowers.

Bulbs in containers

Choose compact varieties of bulbs and soil-based potting mix or reuse the soil in summer containers. Plant the bulbs close together but not quite touching and cover them with twice their own depth of soil. Fill the container to the rim with soil, water it very lightly and put it in a cool place. When the tips of the shoots show through, move the bulbs to the patio. Protect from excess rain or bulbs may rot.

Skimmia japonica 'Rubella'. These are the tight flowerbuds of this male-only form. They open to white in spring. The pollen can fertilize the flowers of female-only forms, such as 'Foremanni'.

Narcissus 'Tête-à-Tête'

Skimmia japonica 'Foremanni'. This form has female flowers only. When planted with a male form, such as 'Rubella', it produces these vivid red berries.

Polyanthus

Variegated ivy (Hedera helix cultivar)

64

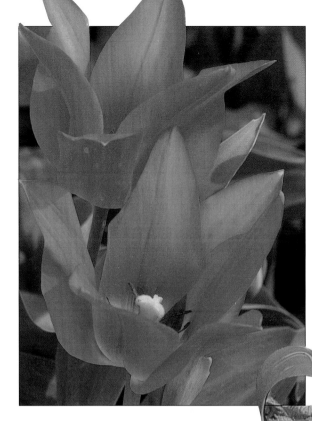

Tulips

Plant bulbs in early fall. If containers are to remain outside during the winter, make sure they have plenty of drainage and are in a place where the soil will not freeze solid.

Above: Tulip 'Toronto' is one of the greigii hybrids and flowers in mid-spring. Unlike many tulips, each stem carries several flowers and they are long lasting. 'Toronto' grows to 12in(30cm).

Primroses

Left: A combination of spring flowers and bulbs with berrying and budding skimmias. A male and female variety are included so that the female plant produces berries.

Left: Tulips often do better in containers than in the garden soil, as they need good drainage. After flowering, it is best to take up the bulbs and store them. Do not leave them in the tub.

Below: A red and pink theme creates a warm color scheme that makes a strong contrast with ivies and green foliage. The plants in this display are miniature roses, begonias and busy lizzies (Impatiens).

The begonias are the larger double flowers, the busy lizzies are single and smaller.

The patio in summer

Summer is *the* patio season: bedding plants, summer-flowering bulbs, patio roses, dwarf shrubs, herbs and perennials all contribute to a riot of color. You can choose a traditional mixture of colors or a scheme based on one or two colors for a more sophisticated effect. Use color carefully; decide whether you want to create a strongly contrasting effect or a gentle harmonizing one. Bright colors stand out best against a contrasting background. In containers you can achieve these effects by teaming bright flowers with colored foliage plants, such as coleus and purple-leaved basil. For a harmonious effect, use similar colored flowers and foliage together - blue, purple and mauve or shades of pink and red. Color can also create an atmosphere. A 'hot' scheme of red, yellow and orange looks tropical and busy, while cool green and white or blue and mauve are still and relaxing. Play with color to make a small patio look bigger. Bright red and yellow plants in the foreground give the impression that they are very close to you. Muted mauves and misty purples at the other end of the patio give the impression of distance. So by grading the colors from hot to cool across the patio, you can create the sensation of space. Heighten this effect by making the patio narrower at the far end than close to the house.

Tuberous begonias

In early spring, plant the corms concave side up in pots and put them on a warm windowsill indoors. Do not water them much until the shoots are well grown. Plant out the corms after the last risk of frost is past. Feed and water the plants well all summer. In the fall, the leaves start turning yellow, which is an indication that the plants are ready to become dormant for the winter. Reduce watering until the stems fall away, leaving dry corms. Dig these up and store them in a dry, frost-free place for the winter. You can then replant them in the following year.

Above: Begonia flowers grow in pairs, a small single behind a large double one. To make the most of the doubles, nip out the singles.

Left: *Fuchsias are one of the most valuable container plants for providing color all summer long. They flower non-stop from late spring until late fall when the weather turns cold. Bring the plants in for the winter in cool temperate climates.*

Right: *A stunning 'cameo' of climbing roses, summer-flowering lilies,* Phormium *(New Zealand flax) and* Convolvulus cneorum *(at the bottom lefthand corner of the picture). The ornamental trellis acts as a frame for the pot.*

Below: *Busy lizzies (Impatiens) are good-value bedding plants that stay in flower all summer. They are most impressive when planted in large groups. Unlike most bedding plants, they will continue to flower happily, even in a shady spot.*

Herbaceous patio plants

Herbaceous plants make a pleasant change from annuals for stylish patio planting. With them, you can recreate a traditional herbaceous border in miniature, or cool, sophisticated schemes based on foliage and flowers. Some herbaceous plants are very suitable for growing in containers - *Houttuynia cordata* 'Chameleon', agapanthus, hostas and *Hakonechloa macra* 'Albo-aurea' are all good - but most fairly compact kinds can be grown in this way, given adequate moisture. The easiest way to grow herbaceous plants is in beds, and a bed next to a patio wall or sunk into paving provides a warm, sheltered situation for some of the more heat-loving kinds. Moisture-loving species associate well with ponds, although they will grow in any bed that does not dry out. Most popular herbaceous plants flower in midsummer, but you can extend the season using spring- and autumn-flowering kinds. Mix seasonal groups together in large beds for continuity of flowering. In small beds or containers, plan each group of plants for a specific season, so that interest gravitates around the patio all year.

Below: Hostas are highly underrated as container plants. Their foliage lasts well all summer, and growing them in pots makes it harder for slugs to find their juicy leaves and nibble at them.

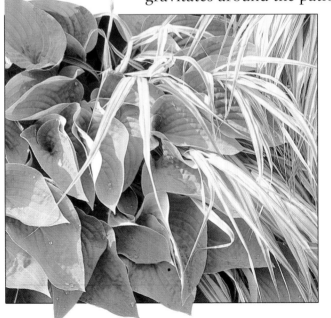

Left: Grasses, such as Hakonechloa macra 'Albo-aurea', and hostas associate very well together. Although hostas are known as shade plants, they will grow well in sun if given enough moisture.

Herbaceous plants for all sites and seasons

In hot spots: hemerocallis, scabiosa, verbascum, dictamnus (burning bush), Sedum spectabile, euphorbia, agapanthus, alchemilla, limonium, incarvillea, stachys and artemisia. Moisture-loving species: astilbe, hosta, lysimachia, trollius (globe flower), zantedeschia (arum lily), and mimulus (musk). For spring color: pulmonaria (lungwort), brunnera, bergenia and dicentra. For late summer and fall color: phlox, Japanese anemones, perennial asters, hardy chrysanthemums, penstemon, rudbeckia, schizostylis, Liriope muscari and phygelius (Cape figwort).

Right: Sun-loving, drought-tolerant plants, such as helianthemum, are ideal for containers in a hot spot, where the soil dries out quickly. This cultivar is 'Beechpark Red'.

Above: African lilies (Agapanthus) are excellent for containers and appreciate the warmth and shelter of a patio. In winter, lag the pots or move them to a cold greenhouse to protect plant roots.

Right: In subdued light, Dicentra spectabilis (bleeding heart) makes a lovely spring show. Both this and its white form 'Alba' look superb against a background of lacy ferns.

A cottage garden feature

An old cottage - or a newer one with a cottage-style garden - would look at home with a patio paved with old stone slabs, cobbles and gravel, and mock Victorian cast aluminum or rustic hardwood furniture. Containers in a good range of sizes and made of natural-looking materials, such as terracotta flower pots, blend in best. Small pots look good in a row along the edge of garden step or on top of a low wall - use them to grow drought-resistant sempervivums, sedums or red pelargoniums. Larger pots suit single specimen plants of fuchsia, marguerite or perennial herbs. You could also plant a mixture of colorful cottage garden annuals in big pots; these can stand alone or be grouped together with other plants. Traditional cottage garden flowers, such as spring bulbs, wild flowers (such as primroses and violets) wallflowers, pansies and stocks are good for spring color. They can be planted in spring just as they are coming into flower. A good range is available in small pots at garden centers ready for planting then.

1 *Choose plenty of different old-fashioned annual flowers and a pair of large matching clay flower pots, one larger than the other.*

Flowers for tubs

In summer, you can choose from a range of old-fashioned annuals, such as clarkia, lavatera, godetia, candytuft, calendula marigolds, larkspur, tobacco plant (nicotiana), verbena and cosmos and combine them with fuchsias, pelargoniums and penstemons to create colorful pots.
For spring color, plant polyanthus, wallflowers, bulbs, violas or primroses. Plant these in fall or in spring from pots.

2 *First plant the biggest and boldest plant towards the center back of the pot as a focal point. Use slightly shorter flowers round it.*

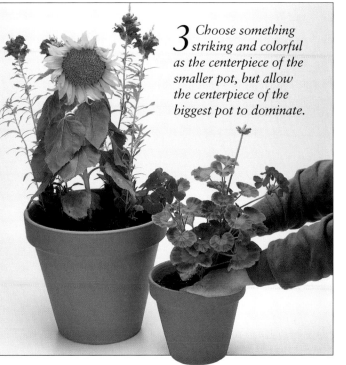

3 *Choose something striking and colorful as the centerpiece of the smaller pot, but allow the centerpiece of the biggest pot to dominate.*

4 Add more flowers, working forwards from the back of the pots, with the shortest at the front. Put contrasting colors and shapes next to each other for a real cottagey look.

5 Finish off with a 'fringe' of low sprawling plants along the front of the arrangement - a row of this type of plant would have been used in an old cottage garden to edge the path.

Snapdragon (Antirrhinum 'Coronette Scarlet')

Dwarf sunflower

Mixed snapdragons

Nicotiana 'Lime Green'

Argyranthemum foeniculaceum

Pelargonium 'Ringo Scarlet'

White alyssum

6 The displays in the two pots blend together harmoniously to become part of the same display. Keep the plants well fed and watered and deadhead regularly.

A Mediterranean display

Patios are relatively new on the gardening scene outside the Mediterranean region, where they originated. There, long hot sunny days and low rainfall meant that instead of cultivating lawns and flowerbeds, it was more practical to have an enclosed yard with paved floor and drought-tolerant plants growing in containers made of local materials. There would also be a vine growing over pergola poles for shade. Today, anyone can create a Mediterranean-style patio at home. White walls, simple garden furniture, a vine - perhaps an ornamental one, such as the purple-leaved *Vitis vinifera* 'Purpurea' - and colorful pots of flowers are the basic ingredients. Red pelargoniums are a Mediterranean favorite, but more sophisticated flowers are just as suitable. Daisy shapes are a good choice - choose blue kingfisher daisy (*Felicia amelloides*), osteospermum or Swan River daisy (*Brachycome*). Succulent plants with thick fleshy leaves look at home here, too. Look for Livingstone daisy (*Mesembryanthemum criniflorum*), lampranthus and portulaca for flowers. Pots of ordinary cacti and succulents can stand outside for the summer for a Mediterranean look. Herbs are also traditional plants of the region. Perennial kinds, such as bay and rosemary, can be grown as specimen plants; pots of bush basil near a patio door are said to keep flies from going indoors. Larger, shrubby Mediterranean-style plants, such as bottlebrush, and potted climbers, such as bougainvillea, can also stand outside on the patio in summer, but as they are not hardy in cool temperate climates, be sure to move them to a frost-free greenhouse or sunroom for the winter. Grow annual climbers up walls and trellis - morning glory (*Ipomoea purpurea*) is very typically Mediterranean.

3 Knock each plant gently out of its pot. Carefully tease out any large roots that are coiled around the rootball, but avoid breaking up the rootball.

2 Plant into any good-quality, peat- or soil-based potting mixture. If the pot is to stand against a wall or in a corner, start with the tallest plant and put it at the back of the display.

1 Select a sufficient number of drought-resistant but non-hardy flowers and herbs to slightly overfill a terracotta pot and arrange them roughly around the container.

4 *Place taller, upright plants, such as this bay tree, in the middle of the container, with lower-growing and trailing plants around the edge, so that they can spill out over the sides.*

5 *Distribute colorful flowers evenly. Tuck in small but dense patches of color to balance up the display's visual impact.*

6 *Try teaming a large planted container with a smaller one, perhaps hanging on a wall. For best results, choose pots of similar style and a complementary color scheme.*

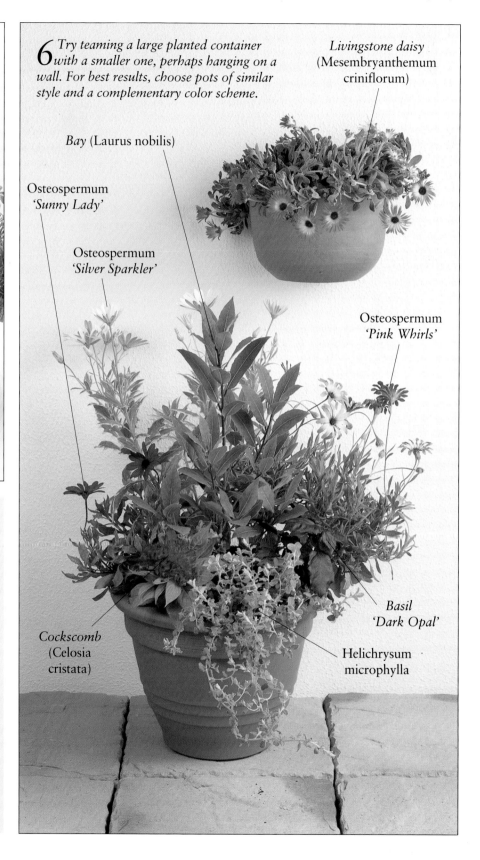

Livingstone daisy (Mesembryanthemum criniflorum)

Bay (Laurus nobilis)

Osteospermum 'Sunny Lady'

Osteospermum 'Silver Sparkler'

Osteospermum 'Pink Whirls'

Basil 'Dark Opal'

Cockscomb (Celosia cristata)

Helichrysum microphylla

A Mediterranean wall basket

1 *Take half a box of Livingstone daisies and plant them without breaking apart the block. Turn it so that the flowers fall over the edge of the container. Plant densely.*

2 *Fill any gaps around the roots with a little more of the same potting mixture. Trickle it carefully down between the sides of the container and the roots.*

A scented pot for the patio

Plant fragrances linger longest in warm, still air, so a patio is the ideal place to enjoy them. Perfumed plants fall into two groups; those with scented leaves and those with fragrant flowers. Of the two, those with scented leaves are most valuable in containers, as the effect lasts longer. Flowers tend to be over in a relatively short time. To release the scent from leaves you must bruise them very slightly, so place the container next to a door where you will brush past the plants or near a seat where you can touch the leaves. Herbs and scented-leaved pelargoniums are the best subjects, as they are reliably fragrant, yet compact enough for pots. Lemon verbena (*Lippia citriodora*), lavender, eau de cologne mint (*Mentha citrata*), pineapple sage (*Salvia rutilans*) and rose geranium (*Pelargonium graveolens*) are the best known. Scented geraniums in other 'flavors' include apple (*P. odoratissimum*), lemon (*P. citriodorum* and *P. crispum* 'Variegatum') and orange ('Prince of Orange'). There are also various spicily scented plants. Try caraway thyme (*Thymus herba-barona*), *Salvia grahamii* (blackcurrant-scented leaves), *Rosmarinus lavandulaceus* (balsam scent), and *Nepeta citriodora* (lemon scented leaves). Pineapple mint has variegated leaves and a mild minty scent.

1 Most scented plants need freely draining conditions - clay pots and a soil-based potting mixture are ideal. Cover the drainage hole in the base of the pot with a large crock.

2 Half fill the pot with soil. Make sure there is room for the plants to stand on top of the soil leaving a 1in(2.5cm) gap between the top of the rootballs and the rim of the pot.

3 Select three scented plants that go well together, and gently tap them out of their pots. Place the first one close to the edge of the pot, turning it so that any overhanging shoots cascade over the side.

Lavender is ideal for a scented arrangement; the aromatic oils occur in the leaves, stems and flowers.

A scented pot for the patio

4 Place the tallest plant at the back of the container, again making sure that its rootball is pressed up against the edge of the pot so that there is room for the last plant.

5 Add the final plant. Choose contrasting leaf shapes, size and texture - include a variegated plant and one that has pretty flowers, as well as scented foliage.

Basil mint (An unusual member of the aromatic mint family).

Scented-leaved pelargonium 'Lady Plymouth'

6 Put the finished display in a warm, sunny spot; in a sheltered area, such as a patio, the scent will linger longest. Avoid overwatering for maximum perfume-power, but do not let the plants wilt.

Lavender 'Hidcote'

Scented flowers for containers

Alyssum
Brompton stock
Bush sweetpea 'Snoopea'
Dianthus
Hesperis matronalis
(sweet rocket)
Hyacinth
Lavender
Some lilies, particularly
Lilium regale, auratum, 'African
Queen' and 'Mabel Violet'
Narcissus jonquilla
(jonquil)
Nicotiana 'Breakthrough'
Night-scented stock
Reseda odorata (mignonette)
Stocks
Wallflowers
Zaluzianskya capensis
(night stock)

Planting up a patio rose

Although climbing and rambler roses can be grown on the patio, up walls and over pergola poles, they must be planted in the ground - in beds of good, deep soil. They will not do well in containers, even large ones, for very long. Only two kinds of roses are really suitable for growing in tubs, namely the patio roses and miniature roses. Patio roses are like compact versions of the larger floribundas and hybrid teas, growing to 18-24in (45-60cm) high. Miniature roses are really small, just 9-18in(23-45cm) high, according to variety, with densely clustered stems. Choose a well-shaped plant with evenly spaced branches, healthy foliage and plenty of flowerbuds. Use a large container and a good-quality, soil-based potting mixture. It is vital to keep potted roses very well fed and watered, as they are growing in a very limited volume of soil. Daily watering may be needed in summer, even if the pot is a large one. Feed every week from the time growth starts in spring until late summer, using a good liquid or soluble tomato feed - unless you can find a liquid rose feed. Prune patio roses in the same way as normal bush roses in early spring (see page 79). Miniature roses do not really need any pruning apart from a light tidy-up in late spring to remove dead twigs. They are not quite as hardy as other types of rose, and are rather prone to winter damage.

3 Stand the plant in the middle of the pot, teasing out any large roots. Fill the gap around the edge of the rootball with more soil.

1 You can use either a clay or a plastic pot, but clay looks better. Cover the bottom of the pot with a good, soil-based potting mixture.

2 Tip the plant out of its pot - if it does not slide out easily, turn the pot on its side and knock the rim gently against something solid.

76

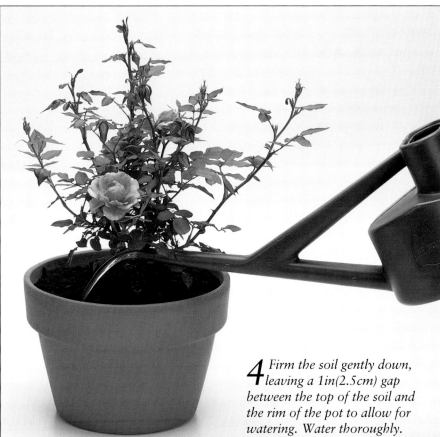

5 *Stand the pot on a matching saucer, which should be in proportion to the size of the pot. Choose one the same diameter as the top of the pot or very slightly larger.*

4 *Firm the soil gently down, leaving a 1in(2.5cm) gap between the top of the soil and the rim of the pot to allow for watering. Water thoroughly.*

This patio rose is 'Ginger Nut', which grows to 18in(45cm).

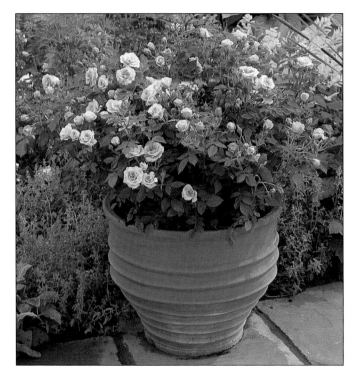

Left: Miniature roses, such as this 'Pretty Polly', have smaller flowers but more of them, and they make more compact growth than patio roses.

Some roses for your patio garden

Anna Ford
Brass Ring (Peek a Boo)
Buffalo Bill/Young
Mistress (Regensberg)
Gentle Touch
Little Bo Peep
Perestroika
St. Boniface
Sweet Dream
Sweet Magic
The Queen Mother Rose

If the potting mixture settles after watering, top it up to the correct level.

77

A selection of patio roses

The very best kinds of roses for pots are patio and miniature varieties, which normally grow 1-3ft(30-90cm) tall. Choose 10in(25cm) pots for miniatures, 12in(30cm) pots for patio roses and 15in(38cm) or even larger pots for compact hybrid teas and floribundas. You can grow the roses in clay or plastic flowerpots, in ornamental tubs or half barrels, but avoid shallow containers, such as troughs. Fill containers with good-quality, soil-based potting mixture. Being low-growing, miniature and patio roses also thrive in raised beds on the patio. You can plant roses in spring or in summer while they are in flower, as long as you do not disturb the rootball when potting them. Keep the containers well fed and watered - use a liquid tomato feed at half strength or a liquid rose feed. Do not let the soil dry out and deadhead the flowers regularly so that new ones are constantly produced from early summer until the fall. Repot container roses into the same pot but with fresh potting mixture every two years at pruning time.

Right: Miniature roses are difficult to place in a garden, but in containers on a patio they really look at home. They 'go' with just about anything, from foliage plants to annuals.

Below: Miniature and patio roses do well in raised beds filled with a mixture of plenty of organic matter, such as well-rotted manure, and good-quality topsoil.

Right: 'Orange Masquerade' is a patio rose that makes a good neat shape in a container. It will produce these intensely colored flowers regularly throughout the summer months.

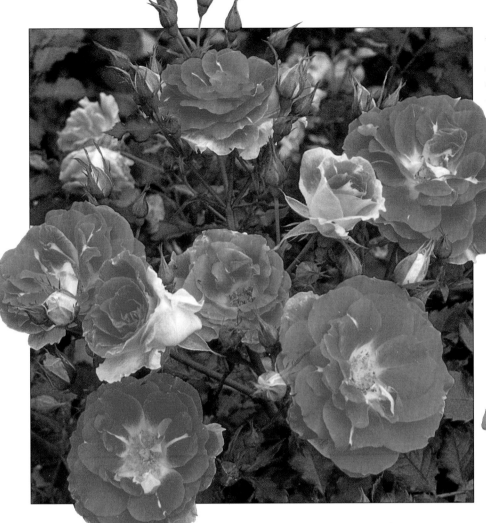

Left: *'Buffalo Bill' (also known as 'Young Mistress' or 'Regensberg') is a compact floribunda rose, suitable for a large patio pot. It has scented, bicolored flowers all summer long.*

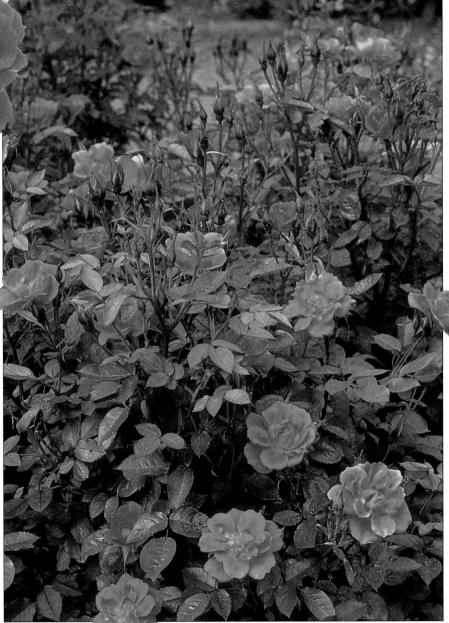

Pruning patio roses

Prune roses in early spring just before new growth starts. (Leave miniature roses until after the worst frosts because their shoots sometimes die back after cold weather.) Remove dead or weak shoots and thin out congested ones in the middle of the bush to improve the shape. Cut back strong shoots to 4-8in(10-20cm) above the top of the pot, cutting just above a leaf joint. Cut the weaker shoots back further than strong ones to encourage them to become more vigorous.

Above: *'Anna Ford' is a patio rose with faintly scented, clustered flowers and robust, glossy leaves. It makes a neat, compact shape and is one of the best varieties for growing in pots.*

A potted rock garden

Rock plants are becoming very popular subjects for containers, with good reason. The plants are small, but with distinctive characters of their own and since few people can spare the space or the time to look after a full-sized rock garden, a potted one is the practical way to enjoy these charming plants. Rock plants naturally associate well together, but be sure to choose plants that share similar growing requirements. Most need a sunny spot and reasonably good drainage, so raise the container up on two bricks so that it does not stand in a puddle of water. Choose plants with different shapes, colors, textures and flower types for the best display. Foliage plants make a long-term background for seasonal flowers. *Artemisia schmidtiana nana* makes a neat silver hillock, and New Zealand burrs (*Acaena*) grow into carpets of pewter or coppery foliage. *Saxifraga* 'Cloth of Gold' looks like golden moss, while *Saxifraga* 'Southside Seedling' has large, tough rosettes heavily encrusted with silver. For flowers, choose a mixture of plants whose flowering times overlap to keep the container colorful from spring to late summer. (The larger the container, the easier it is to have something in flower all the time, as you can get more plants into it). The campanula family have star- or bell-shaped flowers in shades or blue and purple; different varieties flower at different times for about two months. Compact hardy cranesbills are good, too. Small pinks flower in midsummer, as do *Phlox douglasii* cultivars. In smallish containers you will have a better show by planting separate containers of summer and spring rock plants. For early spring flowers grow the pasque flower (*Pulsatilla vulgaris*), *Viola labradorica* and dwarf bulbs, such as *Iris reticulata* and *histrioides*, and *Narcissus asturiensis*.

1 This terracotta pot needs a crock to cover the drainage hole. You will also need some soil-based potting mixture, potting grit and coarse gravel.

2 Put about 1in(2.5cm) of gravel over the crock to prevent soil washing out when you water. It also provides the sharp drainage rock plants need.

3 Almost fill the container with soil. Add some potting grit and mix the two together. 1 part grit to 6 of potting mix is fine for the rock plants in this display.

4 Sink a craggy chunk of rock into the middle of the pot for a realistic background. This is tufa, a type of porous limestone often used with rock plants.

5 *Choose a mixture of plants with long flowering seasons, plus some good foliage kinds. Arrange them around the pot and when you are happy, begin planting. Start by putting in the biggest plants.*

6 *Tuck trailing plants in round the edge. In time, they will soften the sharp outlines. Do not worry if the rock seems to disappear among the plants; it looks most natural if partly concealed.*

Allow about 1in(2.5cm) between the soil surface and the pot rim so that you can add a mulch of gravel later on.

9 *A well-filled container looks fairly mature straightaway. Deadhead regularly and never allow the soil to be too wet or bone dry, as both conditions will stress the plants.*

7 *Finish off by troweling decorative gravel between the plants. This makes a nice 'rocky' surface and holds the plants up off the damp potting mixture.*

8 *Water the plants thoroughly, then wait until the soil is just beginning to dry out before watering again. Scrape away some of the gravel to feel the soil.*

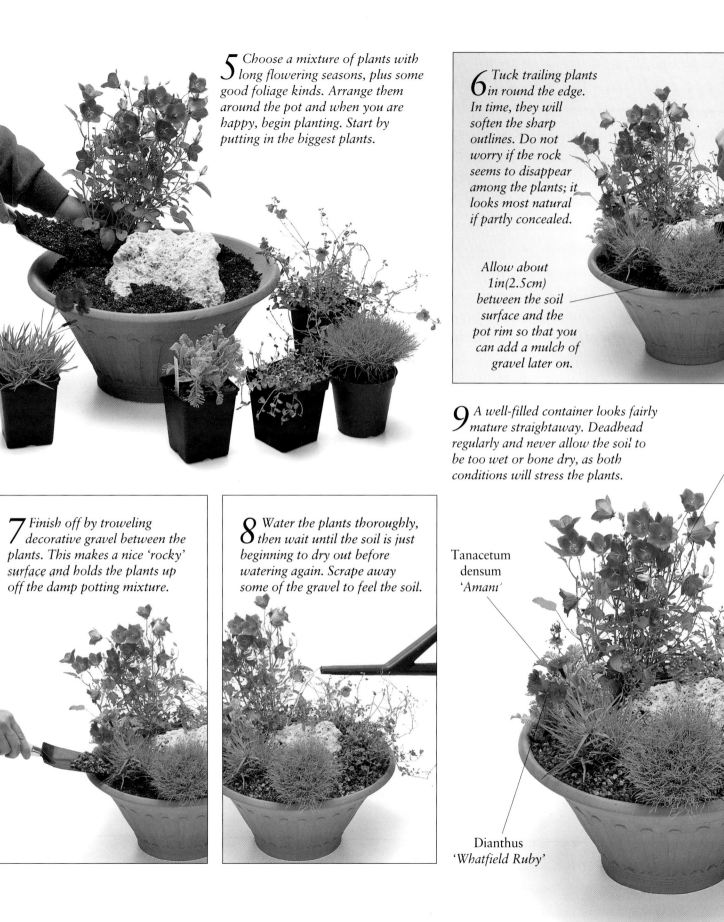

Campanula carpatica

Diascia 'Ruby Field'

Pratia pedunculata

Tanacetum densum 'Amani'

Dianthus 'Whatfield Ruby'

Festuca glacialis

Rock plants on the patio

Rock plants make good subjects for growing in containers on a patio. Neat, compact and often more drought-tolerant than bedding plants, alpines are also very collectable. When buying rock plants for a patio, do make sure that the kinds you have chosen will suit the conditions. Although a lot of rock plants enjoy plenty of sun, warmth and dry air and are easy to grow, not all are so easy to please. Some, such as ramonda, need cool, shady conditions; lithospcrmum and some gentians need lime-free soil, while campanulas and the gentians need to be shaded from searing sun, and moist but open-textured soil from which surplus water can drain quickly. The most drought-tolerant rock plants are those with thick succulent leaves, but others with silver leaves, or very narrow hard foliage, such as thymes and helianthemum, are good, too. These types of rock plant grow best in terracotta pots and troughs, but provided they are not overwatered or allowed to stand waterlogged in winter, you can grow them equally well in plastic containers.

Below: Old stone sinks are popular with collectors for growing and displaying alpine plants; genuine old sinks are scarce and expensive, but cheaper copies made from cement are available. Ensure there are drainage holes in the base and put 1-2in (2.5-5cm) of gravel in the bottom before filling with a soil-based mix with extra grit to improve drainage.

Potentilla verna

Oxalis *sp.*

Houseleek (Sempervivum)

Picea glauca 'Albertiana Conica'

The mounds along the front of the trough are mainly saxifrages. There are many to choose from that will thrive in containers.

Left: Saxifraga oppositifolia 'Theoden' makes a low, tight mat, studded with small flowers in early summer. Give it well-drained soil with some leafmold to retain moisture.

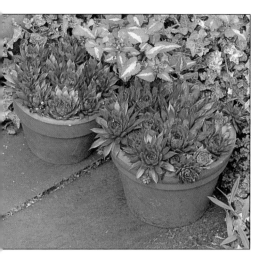

Left: *A collection of the most drought-proof alpines in pots is a good way of decorating steps. Here, sempervivums (houseleeks) flourish tightly packed in terracotta containers. These plants are available in hundreds of varieties.*

Right: *In a sunken bed, created where paving slabs have been removed from the patio, drying out is less of a risk and there is more room to include compact herbaceous plants, such as Sedum spectabile,* geum *(the taller scarlet flowers) and heuchera, along with a selection of rock plants.*

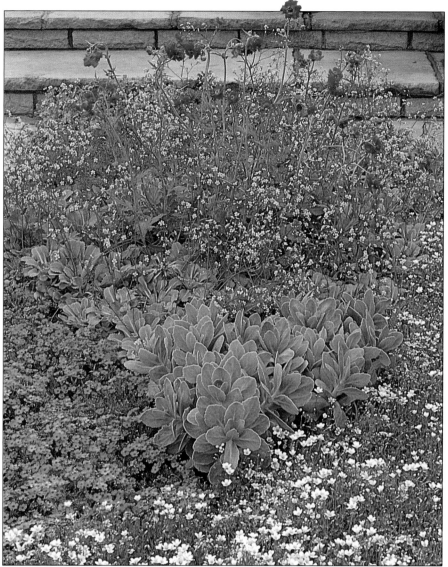

These showy blooms of Lewisia cotyledon hybrids range from pink through orange.

Draba *sp.*

Houseleek

Juniperus 'Blue Star' will stay compact and keep its color.

Gentian

Aubretia

Alpines in a strawberry pot

A small strawberry pot makes an unusual container for drought-tolerant alpines. However, do not forget to water them during dry spells in summer - the potting mix should not remain dry for too long. Trickle water slowly into the pot to avoid washing soil out of the holes.

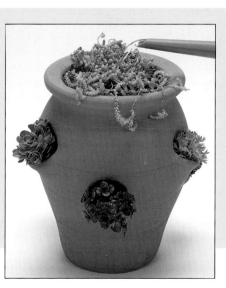

Herbs for the patio

Most herbs are naturally compact, scented and drought-tolerant and they do well in the warmth and shelter of a patio. Being near the house makes them convenient for picking. Very compact herbs, such as parsley, thyme, colored-leaved sages and the various basils, are particularly suitable for hanging baskets, while mints, scented-leaved pelargoniums (some of which are good for cooking), chives, French tarragon and nasturtium or calendula marigold (both of which have edible petals) will grow in containers. Trimmed bay trees or a large group of small-leaved sweet basil make good specimen plants in large pots to stand on either side of a door. You can grow herbs in raised beds and the very drought-tolerant varieties, such as creeping thymes, will grow in gaps made where paving slabs have been removed (see pages 30-31). They do not mind being trodden on occasionally and when they are bruised, they release wonderful herbal scents. Naturally you cannot use chemicals to keep the patio weeded once the cracks are planted with herbs; hand weeding with an old dinner fork or a daisy grubber is the safest answer.

A herbal hanging basket

This hanging basket has planting pockets in the sides. Use soil-based potting mix. Here, yellow mimulus are combined with parsley, golden marjoram, oregano and lemon variegated thyme for a colorful effect.

Below: This is a miniature version of a traditional formal herb garden. It has been planted in geometric patterns, surrounded by an edging of bricks in a gravel path. An arrangement such as this is ideal for a hot, sunny, dry spot.

Plain leaved parsley

Ginger mint

Thyme

84

Variegated lemon balm (Melissa officinalis 'Variegata') with bay and purple sage in front of it.

Golden marjoram (Origanum aureum)

Bay (Laurus nobilis)

Marjoram

Right: *A collection of useful herbs grouped together to make an attractive feature. All but the rue (which is poisonous) have culinary uses - even the lemon-scented pelargonium.*

Three kinds of thyme

Thymus 'Silver Posie'

Rue (Ruta graveolens)

Purple sage (S. officinalis purpurea)

Golden marjoram

Tricolor sage

Thymus 'Doone Valley'

Pelargonium crispum variegatum

Golden sage (Salvia officinalis 'Icterina')

Right: *Feathery chamomile makes a good 'lawn' or path for a well-drained, sunny spot with little wear. Choose the non-flowering clone Anthemis nobilis 'Treneague'.*

85

Planting a cherry tree in a patio container

If you do not have enough room to grow fruit trees in the ground, you can keep them in large pots. Small pots measuring less than 12-14in(30-35cm) are not suitable, as they dry out quickly when full of roots; when this happens, the trees shed their fruit. Apples, pears and cherries growing on a semi-dwarfing rootstock (e.g. Colt) are the most suitable for growing in pots, and figs are superb, as their roots need to be restricted to encourage the plants to crop well. Choose self-fertile varieties of fruit tree unless you are certain that there are suitable pollinators (other trees of the same type but different varieties that flower at the same time) growing nearby, otherwise you will not get a crop. Cherry 'Stella' (shown here), apple 'Greensleeves' and 'Conference' pear all produce a crop when grown on their own. Alternatively, grow a family tree. This is a single tree with several different varieties grafted onto it. Each branch produces a different variety of apple or pear (not both on the same tree), which are chosen to cross-pollinate each other.

Pot-grown apples and pears can be trained as half-standards, bush trees or cordons. Train cherries and figs as standard trees, bushes or fans. Every three years, take the fruit trees out of their pots while they are dormant in early spring and shake most of the old soil from the roots. Trim off 10 percent of the old roots, then repot the plants into fresh potting mixture, either back into the same pot or into a container one size larger.

4 *Add more soil around the roots, firming it down gently. Barely cover the surface of the rootball with fresh soil if you can see any roots showing, but do not bury it deeply.*

1 *Cover the drainage holes of a large pot with crocks. Make sure you can still move the pot once it is filled with potting mixture.*

2 *Add 2in(5cm) of soil-based potting mix. Leave room for the rootball plus a gap of 1in(2.5cm) at the rim for watering.*

3 *Remove the tree from its old pot. Tease out any over-crowded roots. Sit the tree in the center of the new container. Push the canes in around the edge of the pot.*

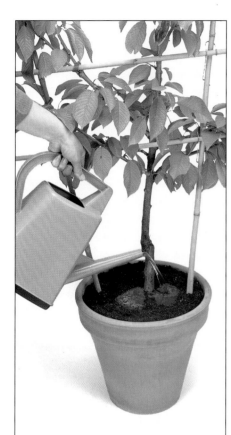

Prune cherries in spring and summer, not in winter.

In summer, cut back overgrown main shoots to a weak side shoot to reshape the tree.

5 *Water the plant well in. A clay pot will dry out faster than a plastic one, so check daily. Do not allow the soil to dry out.*

6 *This tree has been trained into a fan shape. To keep the shape, tie the new shoots up to the supporting framework or they will grow out to the front.*

In spring, cut out any shoots that are growing where you do not want them and tie the rest to the canes. The closer to the horizontal, the heavier the crop will be.

7 *Being flat, a fan-trained fruit tree takes up less room than a normal tree. Stand the pot against a wall or tie the tree to a trellis or fence. The shelter they provide leads to earlier ripening fruit, and makes the crop easier to protect from birds.*

Fruit and vegetables on the patio

Edible crops also appreciate the warmth and shelter of a patio. Fruit trees provide color and interest in both spring and late summer/fall. Trees can be trained as espaliers or cordons against a wall, or left as small bush trees for free-standing specimens. Decorative fruit bushes, such as red and white currants, are easier to protect from birds close to the house. Herbs, compact vegetables and strawberries all make good subjects for pots and hanging baskets, and runner beans look like exotic flowering climbers growing up trellis over a wall. Look for the more decorative varieties of everyday crops, such as golden courgette, purple-leaved basil, purple-podded peas and beans, and the two-tone red-and-white flowered runner bean 'Painted Lady'. They taste just as good as the plain varieties, but look better. In really hot spots, grow heat-resistant New Zealand spinach, tomatoes, eggplants and peppers - they all need plenty of warmth and sunshine.

Below: Ultra-compact bush or trailing varieties of tomato, such as 'Tumbler', are superb for hanging baskets. Tasty parsley makes a frilly 'filler'.

Above: Strawberries grow in special pots with planting pockets in the sides. Pink-flowered varieties, such as this 'Serenata', are decorative, yet produce a good crop of full-sized fruit.

Replace the potting mix and plants every three years to maintain a good harvest.

Right: Stand citrus plants outside in summer, but keep them in a heated greenhouse, conservatory or sunroom in winter. This is the calamondin orange, which produces plenty of tiny bitter fruit, good for marmalade.

Vegetables in pots

Plastic pots do not dry out as fast as clay ones. Fill them with good-quality, soil-based potting mix and plant outdoor varieties of crops, such as tomato. Feed and water regularly; if the crops dry out, they may spoil. Pick the first crops as soon as they are big enough, and pick little and often to keep plants such as beans and peppers productive.

The varieties featured here are tomato 'Alicante', runner bean 'Streamline' and lettuce 'Little Gem'.

Below: Ornamental cabbages are edible, though not as good to eat as normal varieties. However, they are very decorative and newly fashionable plants for late summer, fall and winter color. This simple arrangement of ornamental cabbages in clay pots provides a striking patio display.

You can grow these variegated cabbages from seed, usually sold as a mixture of different colors.

Above: A vegetable corner makes an interesting feature on a patio. Give crops a sheltered, sunny spot and keep them very well fed and watered. You can expect a surprisingly worthwhile crop, even from just a few pots.

Hydrangeas - ideal for a shady patio

Choose a well-shaped plant for instant effect.

The traditional site for a patio is somewhere warm, sunny and sheltered. Most popular patio plants, such as annuals and pelargoniums, thrive in these conditions. But if the only place available for a patio is in shade or if you simply prefer to sit out of the sun, you can still grow some very attractive plants. Ivies are available in a tremendous range, from varieties with curly leaves, leaves like birds' feet, bizarrely twisted and curled leaves, and spotted and streaked leaves. *Ajuga* (low, ground-hugging plants) have purple, bronze or tricolor variegated leaves, with blue flowers in spring. Hardy ferns, with cool, lacy foliage, thrive if kept moist. Hostas come in blue, gold or variegated foliage and make particularly good container plants. Colorful summer annuals are harder to find, but *Mimulus* and busy lizzie flower well in shade if planted after the first flowers have opened. For shrubs, box is happy in shade as long as it gets two hours of sun each day and you can train it into shapes. The plain green Mexican orange (*Choisya ternata*) is happy in shade and has white flowers in early summer. Camellias and dwarf rhododendrons are also good pot subjects, given ericaceous compost, and dappled rather than deep shade. But one of the very best flowering container shrubs for shade is hydrangea. Choose any of the mophead or lacecap varieties and a large pot - at least 15in(38cm) in diameter. Plant blue varieties in ericaceous soil, otherwise they turn a washed-out pink color due to the lime in normal soil. Use normal potting mixture for varieties that are supposed to be pink. Keep hydrangeas exceptionally well fed and watered, as they are gluttons. After flowering, it is normal to leave the dead flowerheads on to protect the young shoots from winter weather. Late the following spring, cut these stems back to where the first young shoot grows out of them.

1 The container should be at least 2-3in (5-7.5cm) larger in both diameter and depth than the pot in which the plant is growing when you acquire it.

2 Plant the shrub into its new container. Use a soil-based potting mixture in the base and to fill the gap between the rootball and the pot.

3 *Sprinkle a little fresh soil over the top of the rootball to cover any exposed roots and protect them from drying out. Or use some bark chippings as a mulch.*

4 *Water the plant well in so that the soil is thoroughly moist. Check the plant daily in summer and water it so that the soil is always very moist.*

Pink hydrangeas can be grown in normal potting mix.

These shoots will carry next year's shoots, so do not remove them during spring pruning.

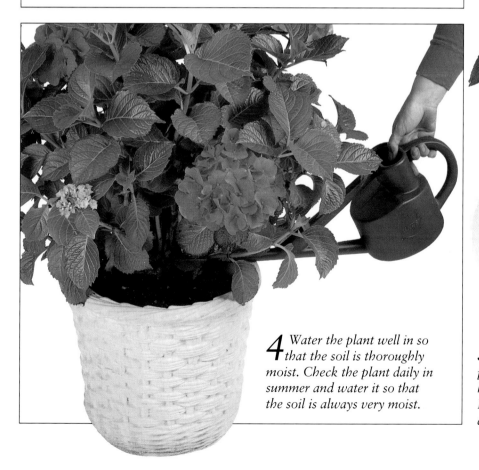

5 *The planted container makes a good specimen pot placed out of too much direct sun; hydrangeas also thrive in full shade. Feed regularly for best results; do not deadhead hydrangeas until early spring.*

Flowering shrubs for the patio

Shrubs can be grown in containers or in beds in the ground, but as space is limited, choose reasonably compact kinds that really earn their keep. Look for shrubs that have particularly attractive or, better still, evergreen foliage, a long flowering season, or fruit and flowers. Or team very compact shrubs with other small flowering plants in, say, a rock garden. Drought-resistant shrubs are good in small containers or in a hot, dry spot between paving. Shrubs can make a low-maintenance, year-round background to containers of flowering plants or they can be the center of interest in their own right. You could plan a bed with one particularly striking plant, such as one of the patio roses, as the centerpiece, with smaller plants - bulbs or ground-hugging plants - growing around it. Look for roses that have been grafted onto a tall stem to give a weeping effect, such as 'Nozomi'. Alternatively, put together a group of shrubs with a range of contrasting colors, shapes and sizes for the best effect. And look out for little-known but spectacular flowering shrubs that will thrive in the sun and shelter of a patio.

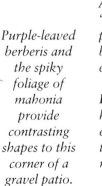

Purple-leaved berberis and the spiky foliage of mahonia provide contrasting shapes to this corner of a gravel patio.

Above: *Dwarf rhododendrons, such as 'Elizabeth', make excellent permanent patio subjects. Choose large tubs - half barrels are good - and a mixture of ericaceous and soil-based potting mix.*

Right: *In a sheltered spot close to a house, camellias will flower a little earlier and the flowers are less likely to be soiled by bad weather. They need the same soil as rhododendrons.*

Left: *A fringe of evergreen shrubs around the patio provides all-year-round privacy and shelter. When not in flower, these rhododendrons provide a superb background for other colorful plants in containers.*

Right: Camellias have become very popular in the last few years, and now a tremendous range of varieties are readily available at reasonable prices. This is the lovely 'Gloire de Nantes'.

A flowering patio

Ballerina apple tree 'Maypole'
Camellias (any)
Hardy hibiscus
(Hibiscus syriacus)
Dwarf rhododendron
Hebe
Prunus incisa *(Fuji cherry) - try*
'Kojo no Mai', a naturally dwarf
form 3-4ft(90-120cm) high
Potentilla
Ceratostigma willmottianum
(hardy plumbago)
Fabiana imbricata
Hydrangeas
Indigofera heterantha,
Callistemon citrinus
(bottlebrush)
Olearia haastii *(daisy bush)*

Below: 'Fuji no Mine', a Camellia sasanqua *cultivar, flowers quite early, in late winter and early spring. It needs a mild, well-sheltered spot with a wall for protection.*

Plant camellias in a mixture of good-quality, soil-based potting mixture combined with ericaceous soil.

Camellia sasanqua cultivars are less hardy than the better-known williamsii hybrids and have smaller, often scented flowers.

An evergreen shrub in an oak barrel

1 *Line the inside of the wooden tub with black plastic, pushed well down into the base. Roll back any surplus plastic over the sides of the container.*

2 *Push the center of the liner out through the drainage hole in the base of the tub. Snip off the tip of the plastic so that water can escape through the hole.*

Evergreen shrubs are very useful all-year-round potted patio plants and a few large, well-shaped plants are always a good investment. They make ideal subjects for growing as specimen plants; try standing a pair of matching evergreens in elegant pots on either side of a doorway in a formal garden. As evergreens are exceptionally versatile and 'go' with all sorts of other plants, you can group them with alpines, smaller variegated evergreens, heathers or traditional bedding plants as background foliage. The most suitable evergreens to use in pots are compact versions of many normal garden evergreen shrubs. Box and bay are useful as they can be clipped into various shapes. Green foliage plants with large, striking leaves, such as *Fatsia japonica* and *Fatshedera lizei*, are handy, too. Evergreens with colored or variegated foliage are particularly useful as they stand out well. Variegated versions of *Euonymus fortunei*, hebe and myrtle are also most attractive. Naturally compact plants such as these can grow in containers for many years without problems. Always choose containers that are plenty big enough for the plants in them and use a soil-based potting mix. Repot the plants into fresh soil every two or three years in spring, just before new growth starts. Alternatively, scrape away the top 2in(5cm) of soil and replace it with fresh material every spring. Keep evergreens well watered and feed them regularly with a general-purpose liquid feed from spring to midsummer. As well as compact evergreens, some larger plants, such as edible fig, eucalyptus, and spotted laurel (*Aucuba japonica*), are suitable, too. They will be dwarfed to some extent as their roots are confined in a pot. However, once the pot is full of roots, they will need much more watering than usual and in practice it is best to grow them in pots for only two or three years before planting them out in the garden.

Use any good-quality peat- or soil-based potting mixture.

3 *Half fill the tub with potting mixture. Choose a suitable shrub: slow-growing or naturally compact types can remain in containers the longest.*

4 *Remove the shrub from its pot by knocking the edge of the container firmly on a hard surface. If the rootball is very tightly packed with roots, tease out a few of the biggest ones before planting.*

If the plant is slightly asymmetrical in shape, lightly prune back any over-long stems or tip the plant slightly to one side to compensate.

6 *Once the plant is positioned correctly in the pot, snip away the surplus plastic from around the top of the container, leaving a strip about 2-3in(5-7.5cm) wide above the rim.*

7 *Roll down the spare plastic to make a 'collar' inside the rim of the pot. This prevents damp potting mix touching the wooden container, which could lead to it rotting.*

Choisya ternata 'Sundance'

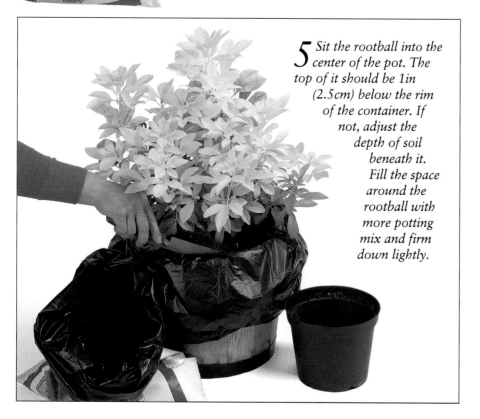

5 *Sit the rootball into the center of the pot. The top of it should be 1in (2.5cm) below the rim of the container. If not, adjust the depth of soil beneath it. Fill the space around the rootball with more potting mix and firm down lightly.*

8 *Water the plant in thoroughly. Check evergreens every day in summer and once a week in winter. If the soil is waterlogged or bone-dry the plants may shed their leaves.*

1 *Give the basket a coat of yacht varnish and then line it loosely with a piece of black plastic to protect the wickerwork from the damp potting mix.*

2 *Half fill the container with moist potting mix or peat. 'Plunge' the exotic plants, still in their pots, into the soil.*

Exotic plants in a wicker basket

Exotic plants with big bold leaves or bright colorful flowers enable you to create a striking tropical look on a patio. Take your cornflakes outdoors on a sunny morning, and it is almost as good as breakfasting in the Seychelles. Good plants to choose for exotic foliage include mimosa, albizia (the silk tree), cordyline palm (*Cordyline australis*) or chusan palm (*Trachycarpus fortunei*). For summer-long flowers, opt for abutilon, standard-trained lantana, or *Salvia grahamii*, which has blackcurrant-scented leaves and masses of floaty red flowers. You could also use exotic fruits, such as lemons, oranges and limes, and most conservatory plants. However, plants of this type are tender, and could not be left outdoors for the winter in cool temperate climates. Keep them in a slightly heated greenhouse, conservatory, sunroom or even an enclosed porch between early fall and early summer.

If you do not have suitable facilities, you can still create an exotic look using plants such as New Zealand flax (*Phormium*), hardy hibiscus (*Hibiscus syriacus*) and *Yucca filamentosa*. These are reasonably hardy when planted out in the garden, but will not be happy left outdoors in pots for the winter, as their roots are relatively exposed. Instead, either put them in an unheated greenhouse, or plunge them in soil up to the rims of their pots in a garden bed. When arranging exotics on a patio, remember that a few well-chosen large specimens will create a more jungly impression than many small ones. And make the most of ornamental pot holders for setting the scene. Rough bark or coconut fiber create the right impression. Alternatively, ordinary rough-textured log baskets or wicker baskets are the answer. Look for old cast-off ones at secondhand sales and give them a coat of yacht varnish. They will last for several years in the garden.

Cordyline australis has dramatic foliage.

3 *Choose a mixture of large, striking plants, including both flowering and foliage kinds. Spiky foliage and large or unusually shaped flowers make a good exotic combination.*

4 Put the biggest or boldest plant into the middle of the group and arrange the others around it. Tuck extra potting mix under the small pots to bring them all up to the same level, just below the rim of the container.

5 Pack as many plants as possible into the container, pressing the pots tightly together. Groups of three or five plants look better than even numbers.

6 Spread a few handfuls of bark chippings or similar mulching material around the tops of the pots. It not only looks good, but also helps to keep the plant roots cool and moist.

7 This arrangement has a maroon theme; each item has a small touch of the same color, which 'pulls together' plants that are otherwise very individualistic in appearance.

Cordyline australis

Hibiscus syriacus 'Red Heart'

Abutilon megapotanicum 'Compactum'

These plants will thrive equally well in a peat- or soil-based mix.

Grasses in terracotta

Container planting schemes need not consist solely of bedding plants. One of the most unusual ideas is to use grasses and their larger relatives, such as bamboos. A large container filled with a mixture of contrasting grasses looks particularly striking in a modern setting, where the dramatic shapes really stand out well. It could also be teamed with smaller containers of evergreens, conifers and heathers to make a fuller display. They all go together very well. Ornamental grasses range in height from several inches up to several feet. The real giants, such as the tall bamboos *Arundo donax* and *Miscanthus*, are best grown in large tubs of their own once they have reached a good size. A row of these makes a good instant screen, which is portable (just) if necessary. But while they are young, they could be used for a year or two in large mixed plantings with other species. Medium-sized grasses suitable for growing on a long-term basis in containers include Bowles golden grass (*Milium effusum* 'Aureum'), *Carex comans* (an unusual bronze form of sedge which, although not a true grass, does looks like one), *Hakonechloa macra* 'Albo-aurea' (a graceful dramatically striped grass with arching gold and green leaves) and *Helichtotrichon sempervirens*, which has wide, ribbonlike, steel-blue foliage. Among the smaller grasses are many species of festuca, which have vivid blue foliage. Annual grasses - the sort grown by flower arrangers for dried seedheads - are not very suitable for containers, as they lack the impact of perennial species, unless they are grown en masse.

1 *Cover the drainage holes with a large crock, and half fill the pot with good-quality potting mixture. Knock the plants out of their pots without breaking up the rootballs.*

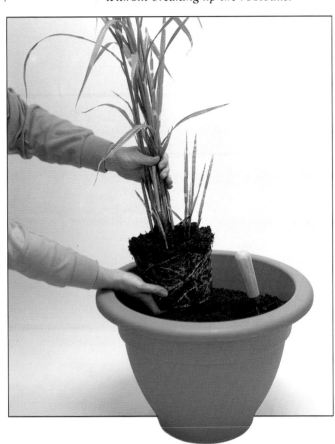

2 *There is only just room in the pot for all three rootballs, so place each one right up against the side of the container. It is easiest to start with the largest plant.*

3 *Tuck the next plant in alongside the first, pushing it well up to leave room for the third. Although space is a bit tight, fill the container well for an arrangement that looks instantly mature.*

4 *Fit in the last plant, squeezing the rootballs slightly if necessary. Arrange any trailing leaves so that they hang over the edge of the pot and are not trapped.*

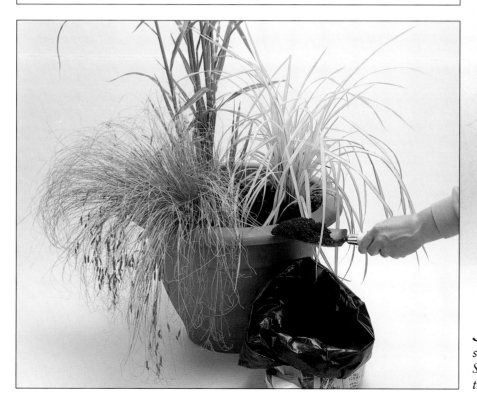

5 *Trowel more soil between the rootballs and firm it down slightly so that it does not sink when watered. Sprinkle a little soil over the tops of the rootballs to cover exposed roots.*

Miscanthus sinensis 'Zebrinus'

6 *After watering in, move the container to its final position. It will look especially good with potted specimen shrubs, particularly evergreens, or standing on gravel, perhaps in an oriental-style area of the garden.*

Bowles golden grass (Milium effusum 'Aureum')

Carex comans

1 *Choose a group of three or five plants with striking yet contrasting shapes, and a set of matching oriental-style ceramic containers - you will also need some cobblestones and gravel to complete the oriental look.*

An oriental-style display

Oriental-style plant associations and containers create a patio that is quiet and restful and perfectly suited to very modern houses and enclosed courtyard gardens. It also makes a good second patio in a family garden, if you want somewhere quiet to escape. Green plants, oriental-style ceramic pots and raked gravel help to create the suggestion of a Japanese garden. Suitable plants include those with striking shapes, such as bamboo, contorted hazel and dwarf conifers. You can include flowering plants, but choose authentic ones, such as ornamental cherry. Look for a dwarf type, such as *Prunus incisa* 'Kojo no Mai' (a dwarf form of the Fuji cherry) for growing in a container. Dwarf rhododendrons, camellias, or a tree peony are also suitable. Add oriental-style ornaments for authenticity - a stone lantern, a miniature pagoda, a granite bridge over a 'stream' of gravel, or water running through a deer scarer - a bamboo pipe that 'trips' as it fills with water and taps a pot. For surfacing, try plain paving slabs or gravel raked into traditional oriental patterns, which are supposed to duplicate the patterns made in sand on a beach by the waves. Add occasional 'stepping stones' of real stone, so you can walk without spoiling the pattern with your footprints.

2 *Place curved clay crocks over the drainage holes in the bottom of each pot, then partly fill them all with a good-quality, soil-based potting mix.*

3 *Knock the plants out of their pots, teasing out some of the largest roots if necessary. Lift each plant into the center of a suitably sized pot.*

5 Spread the gravel evenly over the area, then use the points of a hand fork to 'rake' the sort of patterns you find in an authentic Japanese garden.

6 Add a group of large knobbly pebbles or cobblestones. Press them lightly down so they stay put without looking as if they are sinking.

7 The finished display really creates an oriental look, but the plants do not require the regular trimming and wiring demanded by genuine oriental garden trees.

4 Put the plants in their final position. Spread 1in (2.5cm) of gravel over the area around them, ideally over soil or alternatively over concrete or some other area of hard surface.

Miscanthus sinensis 'Zebrinus'

Cryptomeria japonica 'Spiralis'

Picea glauca 'Alberta Globe'

Bonsai on the patio

Bonsai originated in China many centuries ago. It was developed as an art form and hobby in Japan, where certain types of tree were 'aged' artificially to make them look like the gnarled ones that grew wild in pockets of poor soil in the mountains. Today, bonsai has been taken up by people all over the world. Pine and cherry are the traditional bonsai trees, but all sorts of conifers, deciduous trees and even garden shrubs are miniaturized in this way. Japanese maples, fruit trees, wisteria, flowering quince *(Chaenomeles)*, ginkgo and cotoneaster are all popular subjects. Partly trained young plants are available from garden centers, and both young plants and large, old specimens can be bought at specialist bonsai nurseries. Enthusiasts like to train their own plants from seedlings, but this takes time and expertise. Bonsai are outdoor trees, so only bring them indoors for short spells on special occasions. As they grow in small shallow dishes, they dry out quickly and need frequent watering especially in summer - perhaps once or twice a day in hot spells. A patio is a good place to show them off by arranging the dishes on banked staging or shelves, but make sure they are kept out of strong midday sun and drying winds. In winter, protect the roots from freezing solid by moving the plants to a cold frame or unheated greenhouse during the coldest weather.

Below: A few good bonsai specimens 'make' an oriental-style garden; it is traditional for this type of garden to be in an enclosed space, which provides the much needed shade and shelter for bonsai trees.

Classic bonsai styles include slanting, cascading and upright. Some growers create their own free-style bonsai shapes.

Apply feed
with a hand
spray or a
watering can.

Feeding bonsai trees

Feed bonsai trees every two weeks during the
growing season using a low-nitrogen fertilizer
or special bonsai feed to avoid too much leafy
growth; this one is applied as a foliar feed.

Left: Picea glauca 'Albertiana Conica'
is a naturally compact and very slow-
growing dwarf conifer normally
grown on rockeries, but it is an easy
subject for the bonsai treatment.

Above: An enthusiast's bonsai area,
with a collection of plants attractively
displayed on open staging. The slatted
sides allow good air circulation, but
provide light shade from strong sun.

Patio furniture

Patio furniture should be comfortable, practical and pretty. If you do not have much storage space, choose furniture that can be left outdoors all year round, such as cast aluminum, concrete or hardwood. Store upholstered furniture and soft cushions under cover when not in use, or they quickly deteriorate due to damp. Furniture that stays permanently outside is virtually part of the patio design; you can build seats into alcoves or surrounding walls to save space. For a real 'all-year-round' patio scheme, team this type of furniture with harmonizing containers planted with colorful, variegated evergreen plants. Do make sure that patio furniture is not too big, otherwise it can make the pots and tubs of plants look cluttered, and the area very cramped when you are entertaining. Ideally allow 'occasional' furniture a space of its own, with plants grouped to make a proper display set back a bit from it rather than just dotting them about wherever there is room. To add to your enjoyment of outdoor seating, make sure the patio is well sheltered and gets sun in the evening, when most people make use of their patios. The scent of herbs may help to deter insects, which are often drawn to the lights on a patio on warm evenings. Lamps that burn citronella oil are also a help here - the scent is quite pleasant and it also repels insects.

Below: A formal concrete seat makes an attractive permanent feature in a secluded alcove. In summer, pad it temporarily with cushions. In winter, it makes a pedestal to display plants.

Above: Plastic furniture is relatively inexpensive yet hugely practical. It can be left outside (though best brought in for winter as it blows around in the wind), and is easily wiped clean.

Below: Wickerwork furniture looks attractive but needs storage space as it cannot be left outside in damp or windy weather. An outdoor storage cabinet avoids cluttering up a shed.

Right: Raised hardwood decking with a built-in bench surround. The furniture, too, is hardwood so it can be left out all year round. Perfect for a bird's-eye view of a woodland garden.

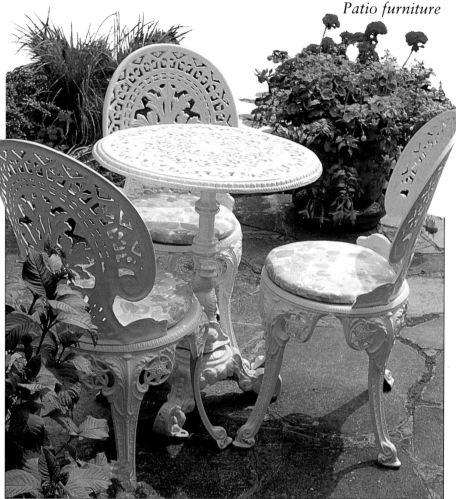

Above: *You no longer need an ancient apple tree to hang a hammock - modern kinds come with their own frame complete with cover; the perfect way to enjoy the garden in summer.*

Right: *Classically elegant versions of popular Victorian designs, originally made of cast iron, now reproduced in cast aluminum. They can be left out all year and are easy to keep clean.*

Routine care

Clean cast aluminum, stone and concrete furniture and containers with a stiff brush, warm water and detergent - not bleach. To restore jaded cast aluminum furniture, remove loose paint and dirt by wire brushing, then apply a special aluminum paint. Hardwood furniture can stay outside all year. Follow the manufacturer's advice on preserving the finish. Put away 'perishable' furniture e.g. basket-weave, after use. Protect hammocks, barbecues and other outdoor furniture with fitted weatherproof covers in winter.

Index to Plants

Page numbers in **bold** indicate major text references. Page numbers in *italics* indicate catpions and annotations to photographs. Other text entries are shown in normal type.

A

Abutilon 34, 96
Abutilon megapotanicum 'Compactum' 97
Acaena 31, 80
  A. glauca 27
Acorus gramineus 'Ogon' *63*
Actinidia kolomikta 59
Aeonium 34
African lily 69
Agapanthus 68, 69
Agave 34
Ajuga 90
Akebia quinata 59
Albizia (the silk tree) 96
Alchemilla 69
Alchemilla mollis 31, 33
Alpines *12, 24, 28, 33, 82, 83, 94*
Alyssum *28, 32, 33, 71, 75*
Ampelopsis brevipedunculata 'Elegans' *54, 58*
Anemones
  Japanese 69
Anthemis nobilis 'Treneague' *85*
Antirrhinum (snapdragons) *33*
  'Coronette Scarlet' *71*
Apples 86
  apple tree *105*
  'Greensleeves' 86
Arabis 33
Argyranthemum foeniculaceum 71
Armeria caespitosum 29
Artemisia 69
Artemisia schmidtiana nana 80

B

Arum lily *11, 40, 69*
Arundo donax 98
Asters 69
Astilbe arendsii 41
Astilbes *38, 39, 69*
Aubretia *83*
Aucuba japonica 94

Ballerina apple tree *93*
Ballota pseudodictamnus 51
Bamboos 98, 100
Banksian rose *59*
Basil 72, 84
  'Dark Opal' *73*
  purple-leaved 66, 88
  sweet 84
Bay *72, 73, 84, 85*
  golden *61*
Beans 88, 89
  runner 88, 89
  'Painted Lady' 88
Begonias *48, 50, 66*
Begonia semperflorens 52, 61
Bellis daisies *64*
Berberis 92
Bergenia 69
Bonsai 34, **102-103**
  cherry 102
  conifers 102
  cotoneaster 102
  flowering quince 102
  fruit trees 88
  ginkgo 102
  Japanese maples 102
  pine 102
  wisteria 102
Bottlebrush *72, 93*
Bougainvillea *58, 72*
Box *62, 63, 90*
Brachycome 72
Brunnera 69

C

Burning bush 69
Busy lizzie *48, 49, 52, 66, 67, 90*

Cabbages
  ornamental 89
  variegated 89
Cacti *72*
Calamondin orange 88
Calendula 33, 70, 84
Californian poppy 61
Callistemon citrinus 93
Camellia sasanqua 93
  'Fuji no mine' *93*
  C. x williamsii 93
Camellias *34, 90, 92, 93, 100*
  'Gloire de Nantes' *93*
Campanulas *46, 52, 80, 82*
Campanula carpatica 46, 47, 81
  C. isophylla 46
  C. portenschlagiana 46
Campsis tagliabuana 'Madame Galen' *58*
Candytuft 70
Cape figwort 69
Carex comans 98, 99
Celosia cristata 45, 73
Ceratostigma willmottianum 93
Chaenomeles 102
Chamaecyparis thyoides 'Ericoides' *63*
Chamomile *32, 33, 85*
  'Treneague' *33*
Cherry tree **86-87**
  cherries *86, 87*
  'Fuji' *93, 100*
  'Kojo no Mai *93*
  ornamental *100*
  'Stella' 86
Chilean potato tree 59
Chives 84
Choisya ternata 90

'Sundance' *95*
Chusan palm *34, 96*
Chrysanthemums 69
  pot *60*
Cineraria bicolor 51
Cistus 24, 31
Clarkia 70
Clematis **54-55**, *54, 55, 58*
  hybrid *54*
Clematis montana 54
  'Hagley Hybrid' *59*
  'Nelly Moser' *54, 59*
  'Niobe' *55*
  'Ville de Lyon' *58*
Clianthus puniceus 59
Cockscomb *45, 73*
Coleus 66
Conifers *13, 22, 24, 34*, **62-63**, *64, 98*
  dwarf *62, 100, 103*
Convolvulus cneorum 46, 67
Cordyline australis 96, 96, 97
Cordyline palm 96
Corkscrew rush 36
Corydalis lutea 33
Cosmos 70
Cotton lavender *27, 51*
Cranesbills 80
Cryptomeria japonica 'Spiralis' *101*
Curry plant *51*
Cymbalaria muralis 33
Cytisus battandieri 59

D

Daffodils *64*
Daisy brush *93*
Dianthus 31, 75, 81
  'Whatfield Ruby' *81*
Diascia 31, 47, 81
  D. cordifolia 46
  'Ruby Field' *47, 81*

Dicentra *69*
Dicentra spectabilis (bleeding heart) *69*
  D. spectabilis 'Alba' *69*
Dictamnus *69*
Draba sp. *83*
Dusty miller *51*
Dwarf reedmace *36, 37*

E
Echeveria *52, 61*
Eggplants *88*
Eichhornia crassipes 36
Equisetum hyemale 36
Ericas *31*
Erica cinerea 'Katinka' *63*
  E. tetralix 'Pink Star' *63*
  E. vagans 'St. Keverne' *63*
Erinus alpinus 33
Eucalyptus *94*
Eucomis bicolor 61
Euonymus 25, 62
  'Emerald 'n Gold' *25*
  E. fortunei 'Harlequin' *63, 64*
Euphorbias *24, 69*
Evergreen shrubs **94-95***, 99*
  variegated *94, 104*

F
Fatshedera lizei 94
Fatsia japonica 94
Felicia amelloides 72
Ferns *34, 38, 40, 44, 63, 69, 90*
  house *34*
Festuca *98*
Festuca glacialis 31, 81
Figs *58, 86*
  edible *94*
Floating soldier *36*
Forget-me-nots *64*
Frankenia 31
French tarragon *84*
Frogbit *36*
Fruit **88-89**
Fruit bushes *88*
  red and white currant *88*
Fruit trees *88*

G
Gentians *82, 83*
Geranium lancastriense 46
  G. psilostemon 59
Geum *83*
Globe flowers *41, 69*
Godetia *70*
Golden courgette *88*
Grapes *58*
Grasses **98-99**
  Bowles golden *98, 99*
  ornamental *98*
Gunnera manicata 41

H
Hakonechloa macra 'Albo-aurea' *68, 68, 98*
Hardy plumbago *93*
Hazel *100*
Heathers *60,* **62-63***, 94, 98*
Hebe *24, 93, 94*
Hedera helix 64
Helianthemum 24, 31, 46, 82
  'Beechpark Red' *69*
Helichrysum 51
  H. microphylla 73
  H. petiolatum 51
Helichtotrichon sempervirens 98
Helxine soleirolii 'Argentea' *51*
Hemerocallis *69*
Herbs *24, 51, 70, 72, 74,* **84-85***, 88, 104*
Hesperis matronalis 75
Heuchera *83*
Hibiscus
  hardy *93, 96*
Hibiscus syriacus 93, 96
  'Red Heart' *97*
Hollyhocks *32, 33*
Honeysuckle *58*
Hop
  variegated *51*
Horsetail *36*
Hostas *17, 34, 38, 68, 68, 69, 90*
  variegated *40*

Hosta crispula 17
Houseleeks *33, 82, 83*
Houttuynia 36
  H. cordata 'Chameleon' *37, 40, 68*
Humulus japonicus 'Variegatus' *51*
Hyacinths *64, 75*
Hydrangeas **90-91***, 93*
  climbing *58*
  lacecap *90*
  mophead *90*
  pink *91*
Hydrocharis morsus-ranae 36

I
Impatiens 49, 66, 67
  'Accent Lilac' *53*
Incarvillea *69*
Indigofera heterantha 93
Ipomoea purpurea 72
  'Spice Islands Mixed' *51*
Iris *38, 38*
  variegated water *40*
Iris histrioides 80
  I. laevigata 'Variegata' *40*
  I. pseudacorus 41
  I. reticulata 80
  I. sibirica 41
Ivy *12, 52, 58, 60, 63, 64, 66, 90*
Ivy-leaved toadflax *33*

J
Japanese maple *22*
Jasmine *58*
Jasminum x *stephanense 59*
Jonquil *75*
Juncus effusus 'Spiralis' *36*
Juniper *24, 31*
  'Blue Star' *26, 27 83*
Juniperus x *media* 'Carberry Gold' *25*
  J. communis 'Compressa' *63*

K
Kingfisher daisy *72*

L
Lamium 'Pink Pearls' *27*
Lampranthus *52, 72*
Lantana *96*
Larkspur *70*
Laurus nobilis 73, 85
Lavatera *70*
Lavender *74, 74, 75*
  'Hidcote' *75*
Lemons *96*
Lemon balm
  variegated *85*
Lemon verbena *74*
Lettuce
  'Little Gem' *89*
Leucanthemum hosmariense 46
Lewisia cotyledon 83
Lilac *35*
Lilies *17, 34, 38, 67, 75*
  'African Queen' *75*
  'Mabel Violet' *75*
Lilium
  L. auratum 75
  L. regale 75
Limes *96*
Limonium *69*
Lippia citriodora 74
Liriope muscari 69
Lithospermum *82*
Livingstone daisies *61, 72, 73*
Lobelia *43, 47, 48, 48, 51*
  'Blue Fountain' *49*
  'Queen Victoria' *37*
  trailing *61*
Lungwort *69*
Lysimachia *69*

M
Mahonia *92*
Marguerite *70*
Marigolds *33, 84*
Marjoram *85*
  golden *84, 85*
Melissa officinalis 'Variegata' *85*
Mentha citrata 74
Mesembryanthemum *52, 61*
Mesembryanthemum criniflorum 72, 73

Mexican orange 90
Mignonette 75
Milium effusum 'Aureum' 98, 99
Mimosa 96
Mimulus 37, 52, 69, 84, 90
Mind your own business
  variegated 51
Miniature bulrush 37
Mint 84
  basil 75
  eau de cologne 74
  ginger 84
  pineapple 51, 74
    variegated 51
Miscanthus 98
  M. sinensis 'Zebrinus' 99,
    101
Morning glory 72
Musk 69
Myrtle 94

N

Narcissus asturiensis 80
  N. jonquilla 75
Narcissus 'Tete-a-Tete' 64
Nasturtium 32, 33, 51, 84
  'Alaska' 51, 61
Nepeta citriodora 74
New Zealand burr 27, 80
New Zealand flax 67, 96
New Zealand spinach 88
Nicotiana 70
  'Breakthrough' 75
  'Lime Green' 71
Nymphaea
  N. laydekeri 'Purpurea' 38
  N. pygmaea 'Alba' 38
    N.p. 'Helvola' 38
    N.p. 'Rubra' 37

O

Olearia haastii 93
Oranges 96
Oregano 84
Ornamental cabbage 60
Osteospermum 72
  'Pink Whirls' 73

'Silver Sparkler' 73
'Sunny Lady' 73
Oxalis sp. 82

P

Pansies 33, 70
Papyrus 36
Parrots bill 59
Parsley 84, 84, 88
Pasque flower 80
Passiflora x *caeruleo-racemosa* 59
Passionflower 54, 58, 59
Peaches 58
  dwarf peach tree 58
Pears 86
  'Conference' 86
Pelargoniums 48, 51, 60, 61, 70,
    70, 72, 90
  'Coco Rico' 49
  ivy-leaved 'Butterfly' 53
    'Summer Shoes' 53
  'Lady Plymouth' 74
  'Ringo Scarlet' 71
  scented-leaved 74, 84
  variegated-leaved 61
Pelargonium
  P. citriodorum 74
  P. crispum variegatum 74, 85
  P. graveolens 74
  P. odoratissimum 74
Penstemon 69, 70
Peppers 88, 89
Petunia 45, 47, 48, 49, 53
  'Express Red Star' 49
  'Purple Pirouette' 53
Phlox 69
Phlox douglasii 80
Phormium 34, 67, 96
Phygelius 69
Picea glauca
  'Alberta Globe' 101
  'Albertiana Conica' 103
Pineapple broom 59
Pineapple flower 61
Pineapple sage 74
Plectranthus 51
Polyanthus 60, 64, 64, 70
Portulaca 52, 72
Potentilla 93
  P. fruticosa 'Red Robin' 31

P. verna 82
Pratia pedunculata 81
Primroses 65, 70, 70
Prunus incisa 93, 100
Pulmonaria 69
Pulsatilla vulgaris 80
Purple-leaved grape 54, 58
Purple-podded peas 88
Pyracantha 57
Pyrethrum ptarmicaeflorum 51

R

Ramonda 82
Roses 56, 58, **76-79**
  'Anna Ford' 77, 79
  Banksian 59
  'Brass Ring (Peek a Boo)' 77
  'Buffalo Bill' 77, 79
  climbing 54, 67
  floribunda 76, 78, 79
  'Gentle Touch' 77
  'Ginger Nut' 77
  hybrid teas 76, 78
  'Little Bo Peep' 77
  miniature 66, 76, 77, 78
  'Nozomi' 92
  'Orange Masquerade' 78
  patio 66, **76-79**, 92
  'Perestroika' 77
  'Pretty Polly' 77
  'St. Boniface' 77
  'Sweet Dream' 77
  'Sweet Magic' 77
  'The Queen Mother Rose' 77
  'Young Mistress' ('Regensberg')
    77, 79
Reseda odorata 75
Rhododendrons 92
  dwarf 90, 91, 93, 100
    'Elizabeth' 91
  miniature 34
Rock plants **80-83**
Rock rose 46
Rosa banksiae lutea 59
Rosemary 31, 72
Rosmarinus lavandulaceus 74
Rudbeckia 69
Rue 85, 85
Ruta graveolens 85

S

Sacred lotus 36
Sage 31, 84
  golden 85
  purple 85
  tricolor 85
Salvia
  S. grahamii 74, 96
  S. officinalis 'Icterina' 85
    S.o. purpurea 85
  S. rutilans 74
Santolina incana 27, 51
Saxifraga
  'Beechwood White' 31
  'Cloth of Gold' 80
  S. oppositifolia 82
  'Southside Seedling' 80
  'Theoden' 82
Saxifrage 82
Scabiosa 69
Scaevola aemula 45
Schizostylis 69
Sedge 98
Sedum 31, 70
  'Lydium' 31
  S. spectabile 69, 83
Sempervivum 61, 70, 82, 83
Shrubs 40
  flowering **92-93**
Silver feather 51
Sisyrinchium 31
Skimmia 65
Skimmia japonica
  'Foremanni' 64
  'Rubella' 64
Snapdragon 33
  'Coronette Scarlet' 71
Solanum crispum 59
Spotted laurel 94
Stachys 69
Stocks 64, 70, 75
  Brompton 75
  night-scented 75
Stratiotes aloides 36
Strawberries 88, 88
  'Serenata' 88
Sunflower (dwarf) 71
Swan River daisy 72
Sweetpea
  bush 'Snoopea' 75
Sweet rocket 75

T

Tagetes *51*
Tanacetum densum 'Amani' *81*
Thrift
 miniature *29*
Thyme *31, 82, 84, 84, 85*
 caraway *74*
 creeping *28, 32, 84*
 lemon variegated *84*
 mother of thyme *29*
Thymus 25, 29, 84
 'Archer's Gold' *25*
 'Doone Valley' *29, 85*
 T. drucei minus 29
 T. herba-barona 74
 'Silver Posie' *51, 85*
Tobacco plant *70*

Tomato *88, 89*
 'Alicante' *89*
 'Tumbler' *88*
Trachelospermum asiaticum
 59
Trachycarpus *34*
Trachycarpus fortunei 96
Trapa natans 36, 37
Tree peony *100*
Trollius *69*
Trollius hybridus 41
Tropaeolum nanum 'Alaska
 Mixed' *61*
Trumpet Vine *58*
Tulips *64, 65*
 'Toronto' *65*
Typha minima 37

V

Vegetables **88-89**
Verbascum 69
Verbena *70*
Vines *11*
Violas *33, 70*
Viola labradorica 27, 33, 80
Violets *70*
Vitis vinifera 'Purpurea' *54, 58,*
 72

W

Wallflowers *33, 64, 70, 70, 75*
Water chestnut *36, 37*
Water hyacinth *36*
Waterlily *36, 37*

'Froebeli' *38*
 miniature *38, 38*
 pygmy *36, 37*
 tropical *36*
Wildflowers *40*

Y

Yellow corydalis *33*
Yucca *34*
Yucca filamentosa 96

Z

Zaluzianskya capensis 75
Zantedeschia *69*

Credits

The majority of the photographs featured in this book have been taken by Neil Sutherland and are © Colour Library Books. The publishers wish to thank the following photographers for providing additional photographs, credited here by page number and position on the page, i.e. (B)Bottom, (T)Top, (C)Center, (BL)Bottom left, etc.

Biofotos: 43(TR), 51(B)
Eric Crichton: Half-title, 10, 12(BL), 32(BL,R), 33(B), 38(L), 42-3(T), 51(TL), 56, 59(TR),
67(BR), 78(BL,BR), 79, 83(TR), 84-85(C), 92, 93(L), 103
John Feltwell (© Colour Library Books): 23(TL,R), 35
John Glover: Copyright page, 11, 12-13(C), 13, 21(BL,TR,BR), 33(TL,TR), 35(BL), 38(B),
39(L,TR), 40, 42, 43(B), 50(BL), 50-1(C), 51(TR), 57(BL), 58, 59(TL,BL), 60-61, 64(R),
65(TL), 66(L), 67(BL), 68-69, 77(BL), 78(T), 82(BL), 82-83(B), 83(TL), 85(BR), 88(BL),
89(B), 93(TR,BR), 102, 104-105
Harry Smith Photographic Collection: 34(BR,TR),39(BR), 41(TR), 65(B), 85(TR), 88(BR)

Acknowledgments

The publishers would like to thank Russell's Garden Center, near Chichester, Sussex for providing facilities for location photography. Thanks are also due to Country Gardens Alfold, near Cranleigh, Surrey for providing plants and containers for photography. Many of the garden design features have been photographed at the RHS Chelsea Flower Shows of 1987-93. The publishers would like to acknowledge the following garden owners and designers: E.C.B. Knight, Mrs. H. Kenison, and F. & G. Whiten.